Write Your Own Script

Live The Life God Has Destined For You

Su Gilstrap

Write Your Own Script

Copyright Su Gilstrap

First Edition © 2017

All rights reserved. No part of this publication may be reproduced, stored in a retrieval system, or transmitted in any form or by any means, electronic, mechanical, photocopying, copy or otherwise, without the prior, written consent of the publisher. We can be reached at sugilstrap.com.

Scripture quotations, noted NIV are taken from the Holy Bible, New International Version, NIV, Copyright © 1973, 1978, 1984 by International Bible Society. Used by permission.

Scripture quotations, noted AMPC are from The Amplified Classic Bible. Copyright © 1954, 1958, 1962, 1964, 1965, 1987, by the Lockman Foundation. All rights reserved Used by permission.

Scripture quotations, noted Voice Trans are taken from Compass Bible Copyright ©2012

The Voice translation ©2012 Ecclesia Bible Society. Used by permission. All rights reserved.

Scripture quotations, noted NKJV are taken from The Holy Bible, New King James Version, Copyright © 1982 Thomas Nelson. All rights reserved. Used by permission.

Scripture quotations, noted ESV are taken from the Crossway Bibles, a ministry of the Good News Publishers of Wheaton, Illinois, U.S.; Apocrypha 2009 by Oxford University Press.

Contents

Foreward by Debbie Kitterman..9

Introduction and How to Use..13

Chapter 1

YOU ARE GOD'S WORKMANSHIP………....……..17

Chapter 2

YOU HAVE THE MIND OF CHRIST......................................20

Chapter 3

YOU HAVE A NEW IMAGE......................................24

Chapter 4

YOU ARE FEARFULLY, WONDERFULLY MADE AND MARVELOUS...28

Chapter 5

YOU ARE MORE THAN A CONQUEROR..............................31

Chapter 6

YOU ARE CROWNED WITH GLORY AND HONOR..............................35

Chapter 7

YOU ARE A RULER..............................39

Chapter 8

YOU CAN DO ALL THINGS..............................43

Chapter 9

YOU ARE AN OVERCOMER..............................49

Chapter 10

YOU ARE A VISIONARY..............................52

Chapter 11
YOU ARE A WARRIOR..55

Chapter 12
YOU ARE VICTORIOUS..58

Chapter 13
YOU ARE FULL OF WISDOM..61

Chapter 14
YOU ARE JOYFUL..65

Chapter 15
YOU ARE PEACEFUL...69

Chapter 16
YOU ARE BLESSED..72

Chapter 17
YOU ARE RIGHTEOUS..................................77

Chapter 18
YOU ARE COURAGEOUS..............................81

Chapter 19
YOU ARE STRONG..85

Chapter 20
YOU ARE FAITHFUL......................................88

Chapter 21
YOU ARE SIGNIFICANT.................................91

Chapter 22
YOU ARE FREE...94

Chapter 23
YOU ARE UNOFFENDABLE..................................97

Chapter 24
YOU ARE HOLY......................................100

Chapter 25
YOU ARE LOVED....................................103

Chapter 26
YOU ARE FILLED WITH GRACE......................................106

Chapter 27
YOU ARE ROYAL HEIRS.....................................109

Chapter 28
YOU ARE CHOSEN..................................111

Write Your Own Script

Decree Page ………….............................……126

Contact Page……………………………………....…….138

Foreword by Debbie Kitterman

Have you ever asked yourself, "What does God have for my life?" Have you ever dreamed of living a life that was full of passion and purpose? Yet, you were not sure where to start?

Well I have great news for you. You are holding in your hands a fantastic resource that will get you on the road to walking in the truth of God's Word, and help you in recognizing His plan for your life.

Su Gilstrap has lived the message of this book, *"Write Your Own Script"* through the highs and lows of life. She isn't just suggesting you do something that might work. She is giving you the tools she knows will work.

Throughout each chapter, Su gives you Scriptural support for the Biblical truth you need to apply to your life today. She also has included verses for daily reading, a thought provoking question, and a decree. That's right -- a decree! The Decrees in this book are powerful and life changing. There is power in our words. As we agree and speak out loud with our own words, the truths that are found in God's Word, we will be changed. We will understand Who We Are and Whose We Are. In writing your own script and living the life you dreamed, you must first get God's view of which you are, and catch His heart and vision for your life.

Psalms 37:4-5 says,

> *Delight yourself in the Lord, and he will give you the desires of your heart. Commit your way to the Lord; trust in Him and He will act.*

As a pastor, speaker, and author, I fully understand the importance of knowing and decreeing God's Word over and into my life. I teach others to do the same in their own life as well.

Su Gilstrap has done the work for you. She has gathered powerful spiritual truths, and given you a tool to apply them in your life today.

In **Write Your Own Script**, Su says, *"If you do the steps in this book, by the end you will be changed. You will be stronger in your knowledge of who you are and who you are called to be."*

As I was reading **Write Your Own Script**, I purposed to do just what she suggests, and so should you. Read the decrees out loud. Proclaim them over your life. Take time to really meditate on each chapter and question.

We are busy people, living in a society that bombards us with many options to suck our time. In **Write Your Own Script**, Su goes on to say, *"You have time to check your texts, email, Facebook, Twitter and Instagram accounts, so you definitely have time to check in with the Holy Spirit. Ask Him for wisdom on how to deal with…"* I have been guilty of letting these things and more suck my time and distract me from connecting with the ONE (Jesus), who has everything I need.

Su has a gift for decreeing and declaring God's word, and it is evident. One of my personal favorite chapters is, "You Are a Visionary." Most of my life I didn't see myself as a visionary. In fact, I would run from it anytime someone would mention it. Yet I am a visionary. It is one of the gifts God has given me, but it is also something God has given you as well. Su says, *"God has put everything in you to be a visionary. Look forward; see the vision for your life, and your family. Grab onto it and don't let go."*

The first step in living the life you want is to focus your attention toward God and His Word. This book will help you do just that! Let's look forward together and begin writing the God given script for our lives.

Blessings,

Pastor Debbie Kitterman

Founder of Dare 2 Hear Ministry

Lead Co-Pastor of Restoration Church

International Speaker and Author, Releasing God's Heart through Hearing His Voice

Lacey, WA

WRITE YOUR OWN SCRIPT

God put "Write Your Own Script" on my heart many years ago. He was showing me that I could live the life I dreamed of when I walked in the truth of the Word of God and my God given authority. But I let other people tell me this was impossible. I went down a road of barely making it, survival mode. It was not fun or comfortable! Then I realized I needed to trust God and not fear or believe the criticism of man. Now with a team of awesome people around me encouraging me to do and be what God has called me to be I have the courage to step out and share this with others.

I felt like God gave me this illustration, "you can write your own script". Just like a writer of a musical or film, He has given you authority over your life and you are called to make it something big and wonderful. This big life isn't a result of leaving things to chance or just waiting for life to happen to you, but you are responsible to cultivate and take action, to obey God's voice in your everyday life and calling. You can write the script of your life, with God's help, you can overcome the things that others have tried to write into your story, things that may have held you back in the past.

To write your own script you must be solid in whom you are. You need to have a strong identity. As a Christian that identity needs to be based in who God says you are, and you find this out by diving into the Word of God, the Bible. What you see with your eyes is not always truth; truth only lies in the Word of God as its base. You continually have to return to the

Truth and see if your thoughts and ideas line up with God's truth, His Word.

I have set this book up as a Bible study, but you can read it anyway you want. I do suggest if you read it as a book, that you go back through the ones that you may struggle with and meditate on the scriptures. I further suggest you write them down and read them out loud to yourself a lot! Yes, it works to get the Word inside of you, God's truth deep down in your spirit transforms you. His Word does not return void, and He sends His angels to accomplish the Word in your life but you have to say it.
For the word of God is alive and active. Sharper than any double-edged sword, it penetrates even to dividing soul and spirit, joints and marrow; it judges the thoughts and attitudes of the heart (Hebrews 4:12 NIV).

Saying the Word out loud consistently in your life and over your life changes you into the majestic person God called you to be! God's word is creative power. When He spoke in the beginning, He created this world and everything in it by speaking. He has told us over and over again in the Bible to speak and create.

"I assure you and most solemnly say to you, whoever says to this mountain, 'Be lifted up and thrown into the sea!' and does not doubt in his heart [in God's unlimited power], but believes that what he says is going to take place, it will be done for him [in accordance with God's will] (Mark 11:23 AMP).

Now we know the will of God because it is written in His Word. He gives us further knowledge as we pray in tongues and He gives us the interpretation. He also gives us wisdom and knowledge of His will in dreams and visions.

Every faith principle and every spiritual law that God put in His Word is for you to live an abundant over the top life!

I have put a decree at the end of each study. The definition of decree is: an official order issued by a legal authority; to order (something) by decree. Synonyms include: order, command, pronounce, proclaim, decide, determine.[1] The reason I used the word "decree" is because of the power of this word. You have legal authority to claim the promise in the Bible for yourself as a child of God. It is a powerful statement with force behind it. You have to see yourself as a legal heir to these promises and stand up and with power DECREE them out of your mouth. You also have to be determined to receive what God has for you. If there is an area that you need to work on then write down this decree and say it out loud several times a day and for as long as it takes to become firm in your spirit. I also included the decrees all in one place at the back of the book. So if you want to just go back over the decrees it will be easy for you.

If you will do the steps I line out for you in this book, by the end you will be changed. You will be stronger in your knowledge of who you are and who you are called to be. You will have a solid
Foundation of who God created you to be!
He loves us so much and wants you to have the very best life. He also needs us firm in who He called us to be, to tell His good news to the world and usher in heaven on earth.
Let's get started!

---

[1] Google.com

Write Your Own Script

ONE

YOU ARE GOD'S WORKMANSHIP

> *For we are God's workmanship, created in Christ Jesus unto good works, which God prepared in advance for us to do Ephesians 2:10 ESV).*

> *For we are God's [own] handiwork (His workmanship), recreated in Christ Jesus, [born anew] that we may do those good works which God predestined (planned beforehand) for us [taking paths which He prepared ahead of time], that we should walk in them [living the good life which He Prearranged and made ready for us to live] (Ephesians 2:10 AMPC).*

The Greek definition of *workmanship* is: what has been made, of the works of God as creator.[2]

The Greek definition of *create* is: form, shape, make, always of God.[3]

---

[2] Strong's Concordance, Bible Hub: Search, Read, Study the Bible in Many Languages. ©2004-2016 by Bible Hub.
[3] Strong's Concordance, Bible Hub: Search, Read, Study the Bible in Many Languages. ©2004-2016 by Bible Hub.

The Greek definition of *in* is: inside, in which something operates from the inside.[4]

Notice the definition of the word "*in*", it says, "In which something operates from the inside." The verse says we are created *in* Christ Jesus unto good works. So we are created *in* (in which something operates from the inside) of Christ Jesus unto good works. We operate from inside Christ Jesus unto good works. So we are inside of Christ! We are working from inside of His wisdom, knowledge, and all of the fruits of His Spirit.

These things aren't just out there to grasp, but we are on the inside! They are in us and we are in them. When we are born again we look like, talk like, think like, and act like Jesus. We are His workmanship (of the works of God as creator)! Meditate on this; let it get way down in your spirit so you live from this place. When you are saved you are now a new creature in Christ Jesus.[5]

Your spirit is born again, it is new, but you have to renew your mind to catch up with your newness in the Spirit. How do you renew your mind? Doing what you are doing right now, putting the Word in, and saying it out loud. Reprogramming, putting new information in, this is how you bring your mind up to where your spirit is.

So when you think about yourself now what are you going to say? That you missed the mark? That you aren't enough? That you aren't loveable? **NO**, you will say, **"I am God's workmanship"**. I am His

---

[4] Strong's Concordance, Bible Hub: Search, Read, Study the Bible in Many Languages. ©2004-2016 by Bible Hub.
[5] 2 Corinthians 5:17

handiwork. I operate from within Jesus Christ and His anointing. I am taking the path God created for me in advance, living the good life He prearranges for me to live.

Some people think being down on yourself is being humble. This is completely untrue! Speak what God says about you, which is always positive and always forward motion.

> *I do not consider, brethren, that I have captured and made it my own [yet]; but one thing I do [it is my one aspiration]: forgetting what lies behind and straining forward to what lies ahead, I press on toward the goal to win the [supreme and heavenly] prize to which God in Christ Jesus is calling us upward (Philippians 3:13-14 AMPC).*

You are plenty! You are enough! You will succeed! You are God's handiwork and He has laid out a successful, fantastic life for you to live. Believe it, say it, walk it out.

DECREE: I am God's workmanship; I am created by God, the Creator of the universe! I operate from the Holy Spirit; I have the mind of Christ and walk in His truth. I am enough, I am worthy, and I will reach my goals!

Daily Read: Psalms 1

Think about it! As you look at yourself today, think about how you are created in God's image, His exact likeness. What one thing about yourself are you going to thank God for today?

TWO

YOU HAVE THE *MIND* OF CHRIST

> *For who has known the mind of the Lord that he may instruct him? But we have the mind of Christ (1 Corinthians 2:16 NIV).*
>
> *For who has known or understood the mind (the counsels and purposes) of the Lord so as to guide and instruct Him and give Him knowledge? But we have the mind of Christ (the Messiah) and do hold the thoughts (feelings and purposes) of His heart (1 Corinthians 2:16 AMPC).*

The Greek definition of *have* is: possess, ability, keeping, maintaining, obtained, retain.[6]
The Greek definition of *mind* is: understanding, reasoning, the reason, the reasoning faculty, intellect.[7]

> *I no longer call you servants, because a servant does not know his master's business. Instead, I have called you friends, for*

---

[6] Strong's Concordance Bible Hub: Search, Read, Study the Bible in Many Languages.© 2004-2016 by Bible Hub
[7] Strong's Concordance Bible Hub: Search, Read, Study the Bible in Many Languages.© 2004-2016 by Bible Hub

everything that I learned from my Father I have made known to you (John 15:15 NIV).

So as Christians, with born again spirits, we have the *mind* of Christ. Believe this, this is Truth.
I hear so many people say they can't hear God, or God isn't talking to me, but He is, He is constantly talking to us, and He is inside you. He is inside of you, not far off. You just need the time to sit and hear Him and to start recognizing His voice.

The Bible says we possess the ability to keep maintaining the understanding and reasoning of Christ.[8] Jesus has given us *everything* that He learned from God the Father.[9] Think about this! Meditate on it until it gets as solid as a rock foundation. You need to have this right there in your pocket. When the devil tries to come and lie to you and tell you don't know what to do, you whip this out of your pocket and say ah ha! Yes I do because I have the mind of Christ which is the wisdom and knowledge of God!

You are brilliant! You have the mind of Jesus! You can figure out mysteries, come up with the needed business plan, raise your children, stay married, move forward in your life. It's all right there inside of you.

Now the best, fastest way to walk in this wisdom is to put the Word in you constantly and ask the Holy Spirit to show you the truth you need to know. Psalm 1:2 says to meditate on the Word day and night. One way to do this is to have either the Bible being read out loud by a Bible app or you can go to YouTube

---

[8] 1 Corinthians 2:16
[9] John 15:15

Write Your Own Script

and find many affirmation or scripture reading videos. I play these on low volume all night long.

You have to put more truth in than worldly wisdom. Is this overkill? I don't know, how bad do you want to move forward in life? How bad do you actually want the things that the Bible promises you? How bad do you actually want to live in freedom, joy, and peace? How bad do you actually want to do the things God is calling you to do? You get to choose, but don't put the blame on God and say He's not talking to you. Plain and simple, if you don't hear God you're not listening close enough or you haven't trained your spirit to know His voice.

The Bible says to think on these things, *"whatever is true, noble, right, pure, whatever is lovely, whatever is admirable if anything is praiseworthy or excellent think about such things"*, *(Philippians 4:8).*
I'm pretty sure at least half of what is on social media or television does not fulfill these criteria. Or how about the music you listen to? Not to put the finger on a touchy subject, but you will be what you feed your mind with. **You get to choose.**

You know how a computer needs to be programed with the right information for you to be able to retrieve it? Well we need to open up our spirit to be reprogrammed by the Holy Spirit and the Word, which is Christ.[10] So when it says we have the mind of Christ, and Jesus Christ is the Word, meditating on it is how you yield fruit. It's how we bring up the wisdom that is in our spirit, once we are saved and the Spirit of God lives in us.

I am not saying never watch television or get on Facebook again. What I am saying is to be

---

[10] John 1:1

intentional about putting more of the Word and the truth in than these distractions. If you want to fully walk in the spectacular life God has planned for you, you have to follow His plan book. So if you are to follow the plan you have to know the plan.

To sum up, when we are saved by asking Jesus into our life and receiving the Holy Spirit we are filled with His mind. Our spirit knows the truth but our minds have to be renewed to access the information. Renewing our mind is easy! It simply takes us putting in the information which is the Word. Praying in the Spirit will help you retrieve the Word and the wisdom God has for you.

Determine in your heart today to reprogram your mind so you can access the wisdom of God that He freely gives to you. God is not trying to hide from you or keep anything from you. He is for you and wants you to succeed.

DECREE: I have the mind of Christ. I have the wisdom of God, which He freely gives to me as His beloved child. I will put in the Word, which is Christ and renew my mind daily to walk in His truth and wisdom. I hear the voice of the Lord and will incline my ear to His voice. I choose to walk with the Spirit of God.

Daily Read: Proverbs 4:6-7

Think About it: How am I going to put God and His Word and wisdom first place in my life today?

THREE

YOU HAVE A NEW *IMAGE*

> *Do not lie to one another, since you have put off your old man with his deeds, and have put on the new man, who is being renewed in knowledge according to the image of Him who created him (Colossians 3:9-10 NKJV).*
>
> *For you have stripped off the old (unregenerate) self with its evil practices, and have clothed yourselves with the new [spiritual self], which is [ever in the process of being] renewed and remolded into [fuller and more perfect knowledge upon] knowledge after the image (the likeness) of Him Who created it (Colossians 3:9-10 AMPC).*

The Strong's Concordance says this about the word *renew*: this word only occurs in 2 Corinthians 4:16 and Colossians 3:10 both times referring to God ever transforming the believer by the renewing "the new man" in Christ.[11]

---

[11] Strong's Concordance
Bible Hub: Search, Read, Study the Bible in Many

The dictionary gives this definition of renew: to make (something) new, fresh, or make strong again: to make (a promise, vow, etc.) again: to begin (something) again especially with more force or enthusiasm.[12]

Many of us when we come to finally accept Jesus as our Savior are not super proud of whom we used to be. Some of us have done embarrassing or just plain terrible things. We wish we could undo or forget what we did and where we came from. We want a start over. And you absolutely can! God has given us all the tools and the knowledge and the supernatural help we need to be made into a new glorious image that looks and acts just like Jesus. You probably won't arrive at completion overnight. In fact it will take a lifetime of continually being made more like Him. But you do in fact have the ability to have a brand new image of Christ likeness today.

How do we cultivate this more and more? You put the Word in, you say the Word, sing the Word, pray the Word, read the Word. The Word (the Bible), going in your eyes and out of your mouth will bring life and change to you and the circumstances around you. It is supernatural and alive.
The Bible isn't just a book; it is supernatural and will change you as you say it out of your mouth believing it will work for you.

> *Let us then fearlessly and confidently and boldly draw near to the throne of grace (the throne of God's unmerited favor to us sinners), that we may receive mercy [for our failures] and find grace to help in good time*

Languages. © 2004-2006 by Bible Hub
[12] Google.com

> *for every need [appropriate help and well-timed help, coming just when we need it] (Hebrews 4:14 AMPC).*

In Genesis it says that humans were made in the image of God. Adam screwed that up, but Jesus bought this back for us, with His blood. It's up to us to become who He created us to be. He has sent us a Helper, the Holy Spirit. As we are filled daily with power from the Holy Spirit and renew our mind with the Word we take on more and more of Christlikeness. Until the day of redemption we will be becoming more like Him, If we daily press in to know Him more.

Yes it takes you making an effort. It takes you putting in the time in the secret place to get alone with God. It takes time in the prayer closet pursuing Him and His answers for your life. It takes you reading the Word, memorizing the Word, saying it out your mouth, seeing it with your eyes. It takes you staying in community with other believers who believes the truth of the Word! Yes it takes some work on your part but He gives so much more!

You will never be the same again.
You will:
- **Break strongholds!**
- **Walk out of poverty!**
- **Stop being a victim!**
- **Walk out of unworthiness!**

And now... walk into a fabulous new life that God has created for you! The tradeoff is definitely worth it!

DECREE: I am being ever transformed in the knowledge of Christ. I am being created in the image of God from glory to glory by the Spirit of the Lord. As I renew my mind to understand who I am in Christ, I will be changed into God's image on the inside and outside as well.

Daily Read: Ephesians 4:22-24

Think About It: What stronghold will you break today? Tell it to go, in Jesus' mighty Name! Find the Word for renewal and stand!

FOUR

YOU ARE *FEARFULLY, WONDERFULLY* MADE, AND *MARVELOUS*

> *I will praise You, for I am fearfully and wonderfully made; marvelous are Your works, and my soul knows very well (Psalms 139:14 NKJV).*

The definition for *fearfully:* inspire reverence, Godly fear, and awe.[13]

The definition for *wonderfully:* distinguished, make a distinction, set apart.[14]

The definition for *marvelous:* be surpassing or extraordinary, wonderful.[15]

Different commentaries and versions of the Bible put the emphasis of the words fearfully and wonderfully either on the creation or the creator. Either to describing God or describing His creation, us! For

---

[13] Brown-Driver-Briggs Hebrew and English Lexicon Unabridged Electronic database. Copyright 2002, 2003, 2006 by Biblesoft, Inc.

[14] NAS Exhaustive Concordance of the Bible with Hebrew-Aramaic and Greek Dictionaries Copyright 1981, 1988 by The Lockman Foundation

[15] Brown-Driver-Briggs Hebrew and English Lexicon Unabridged Electronic database. Copyright 2002, 2003, 2006 by Biblesoft, Inc.

this study we are going to use the emphasis on us, His creation.

In Genesis it says we are created in God's image, we have His attributes, that alone is something to dance about! Then in this scripture, " fearfully" means to inspire reverence and awe. Can you imagine when God made humans and the devil saw them and who they were like? He got so jealous and hated them instantly. Then he realized that God gave them the same creative power He had. Wow! So Satan totally gets this, how about Christians realizing who they are now.

As saved Christian you have the Spirit of the **living God inside** of you! As you walk with the Holy Spirit and in His power you will inspire reverence and awe of God to those around you, and the fear of God to demons. They will see that you walk in the authority of Jesus if you believe you do!

You are also wonderfully made, distinguished and set apart for a distinct purpose. God on purpose created you for a unique life that is to be extraordinary! Do you believe this?

Don't let your circumstances or any naysayer around you tell you differently. It only takes a change of heart and mind.

This is not prideful thinking. Being humble is not thinking less of yourself, being humble is thinking highly of others. Also when you love yourself you can authentically love others. If you do not love yourself you will not be able to love others.

Once you change your mind and your perception of who you are, your life will dramatically change. When you realize you were created distinctly and extraordinary you will live a life on purpose and with great hope in your future. When you understand how God sees you and how much He loves you and how great He thinks you are you will be able to do anything!

Decree: I am fearfully made; I inspire reverence to God everywhere I go. I am distinguished, set apart, for Your kingdom, Lord. I am marvelously and extraordinarily made! I am God's workmanship. Created in His exact image. He created me with a passion to fulfill a purpose on the earth. I believe this; I choose this day to walk in this truth.

Daily Read: Genesis 1:27 and Ephesians 2:10 (Read through this verse in the Amplified version, so good!)

Think About It: Think about your purpose, your passion. What drives you? Write this down and ask God to make this real to you!

FIVE

YOU ARE MORE THAN A *CONQUEROR*

> *Yet amid all these things we are more than conquerors and gain a surpassing victory through Him Who loved us (Romans 8:37 AMPC).*

The Greek definition for *conqueror* is: prevail mightily, completely and overwhelmingly victorious, surpassing victory, prevail completely.[16]
The Greek definition for *through* is: on account of, because of, this is the reason why.[17]

Restating the verse with these definitions-- you can say that, "You prevail mightily, completely and you are overwhelmingly victorious and prevail completely through Jesus, the One Who loves you!"

> *For whatever is born of God is victorious over the world; and this is the victory that conquers the world, even our faith (1 John 5:4 AMPC).*

How many times do you walk through your day feeling defeated or like a failure? Or maybe you feel like you will never quite measure up? Do you have huge obstacles in your life that you are trying to

---

[16] Helps Word Studies copyright 1987, 2011 by Helps Ministries, Inc.
[17] Strong's Concordance

overcome and maybe feeling hopeless? I have the answer!

The answer is that we are always victorious through Jesus! You win!

God has already given you everything you need to accomplish your best life. Does this sound too easy? I'm not saying it's going to fall at your feet. You are going to have to put an effort into it. Reading and meditating on the Word, spending time sitting at Jesus' feet, praying in the Spirit, seeking wisdom. But as you do these things there will be a super on your natural and you will be a conqueror. It may not be quick or easy, but it is simple.

How do you accomplish this feat? With your faith in Jesus and His Word and by believing what and who He says you are.

> *But thanks be to God, who gives us the victory through our Lord Jesus Christ (1 Corinthians 15:57 NIV).*

You build up your faith by reading, saying, and hearing the Word. This has to be more than once a week in church. You have to decide you are all in. One person I was talking to about this said, "oh, you mean I have homework?" Yes, you do! Turn off the television, get off social media, and make the Word of God first priority. Invest yourself and your time in the Word and you will reap great dividends in every area of your life.

> *Consequently, faith comes from hearing the message, and the message is heard through the word of Christ (Romans 10:17 NIV).*

The word that is used in the original text for hearing in this verse means to hear and hear and keep on hearing. So read it over and over, say it over and over. This builds up and makes a firm foundation of faith in your spirit.

> *But you, beloved, building yourselves up on your most holy faith, praying in the Holy Spirit, keep yourselves in the love of God, looking for the mercy of our Lord Jesus Christ unto eternal life (Jude 1:20 NKJV).*

Find the scriptures that you need to stand on for what you need in your life.

What do you need?
- **Wisdom?**
- **Healing?**
- **Financial breakthrough?**
- **Relationship help?**

Or any number of situations that life is throwing at you. You can find the answer in the Word. Find scriptures for each situation and read them, say them, hear them constantly until it builds up your faith.

When you are baptized with the Holy Spirit and receive a new tongue, a heavenly language, praying with this allows a direct line to God without Satan knowing what you are saying. This is good news!

> *So too the [Holy] Spirit comes to our aid and bears us up in our weakness; for we do not know what prayer to offer nor how to offer it worthily as we ought, but the Spirit Himself goes to meet our supplication and pleads in our behalf with unspeakable yearnings and*

Write Your Own Script

> *groaning's too deep for utterance (Romans 8:26 AMPC).*

When you need to conqueror something in your life pray in the Holy Spirit, find scriptures on what you are dealing with, write them down, memorize them, decree them over your life. Do not speak what you have, speak what you need or want.

> *For assuredly, I say to you, whoever says to this mountain, "Be removed and be cast into the sea," and does not doubt in his heart, but believes that those things he says will be done, he will have whatever he says. Therefore I say to you, whatever things you ask when you pray, believe that you receive them, and you will have them (Mark 11: 23-24 NKJV).*

DECREE: I am a conqueror through Jesus my Lord. I prevail mightily and am overwhelmingly victorious. I will prevail completely over every problem and enemy in my life. Thank you God for always giving me the victory. I will build up my faith with the Word and praying in the Spirit today.

Daily Read: Isaiah 54:13-17

Think About It: What is one Scripture you can stand on this week that will bring victory in one area of your life?

SIX

YOU ARE CROWNED WITH *GLORY* AND *HONOR*

> *Yet You have made him but a little lower than God [or heavenly beings], and You have crowned him with glory and honor (Psalms 8:5 AMPC).*

The Hebrew definition for God [heavenly beings] is: Elohim- which means God, divine, judges, and ruler.[18]
The definition for crowned is: compass, to encircle (for attack protection).[19]
The definition of glory is: honor, abundance, riches, of external condition and circumstances.[20]
The Hebrew definition of honor is: an ornament, beautiful, dignity, majestic, majesty, and splendor.[21]

---

[18] Strong's Concordance, Bible Hub: Search, Read, Study the Bible in Many Languages © 2004-2016 by Bible Hub
[19] Strong's Exhaustive Concordance, Bible Hub: Search, Read, Study the Bible in Many Languages © 2004-2016 by Bible Hub
[20] Brown-Driver-Briggs Hebrew and English Lexicon, Unabridged, Electronic Database.
Copyright 2002, 2003, 2006 by Biblesoft, Inc.
[21] Strong's Concordance, Bible Hub: Search, Read, Study the Bible in Many Languages © 2004-2016 by Bible Hub

Write Your Own Script

You have been created a little lower than God, the divine and He has crowned or encircled you with favor, abundance, riches, richness of external condition and circumstances and with beauty, dignity, majesty and splendor.

Wow! Do you see yourself in this way? Do you walk with your head up as if you are royalty? Read through the statement above, again and speak it out loud. Do you believe it? What would it look like if you thought of yourself as royalty?

I have seen royalty from time to time and I always think how dignified and graceful and self-assured they present themselves. If we as God's kids were assured of who we are in Him we would walk this way in our life. Then in turn, because we are confident in who we are and know we are loved we will love others. If you do not look at life with a victim attitude you can love better and more fully.

> *Because you are precious in My sight and honored and because I love you (Isaiah 43:4a AMPC).*

The word, " precious" in this verse means: to be prized, esteemed, or valued.[22]
Honored means: respected, distinguished, and glorious.[23]

You can see in these two verses that God loves you, honors you, esteems you, He values you and wants to surround you with riches, abundance, splendor. And on and on! Do you get this? God is not out to

---

[22] Strong's Concordance, Bible Hub: Search, Read, Study the Bible in Many Languages © 2004-2016 by Bible Hub.
[23] Google.com

punish you or make your life miserable! Satan is. Satan comes to steal, kill and destroy you. God has come to give you life and life abundantly.[24]

Religious tradition has taught many that God uses pain, disasters, takes loved ones and makes your life generally unbearable to teach you lessons to become better. This is so untrue. God is a good, good God and loves you so much and only wants the best for you. The statement that so many quote, "God is more interested in your character than your comfort", is usually quoted to people who are really having a tough time, which says to them, God wants you miserable to teach you something. I'm not arguing that God is interested in building your character, but it is not through pain and destruction.

> *James 1:3 says, "When tempted, no one should say, "God is tempting me. For God cannot be tempted by evil, nor does He tempt anyone".*

We will have trials, *John 16:33 says, "but be of good cheer; I have overcome the world".* We will have trials, BUT GOD! My God, your God has overcome it all already. God has taken care of it, He has defeated Satan and if we walk in His wisdom and His right way of doing things we will be overcomers too.

We have **all** of **God's power** behind us; we just need to use it.
- **Read the Word.**
- **Decree the Word.**
- **Memorize the Word.**
- **Believe the Word.**
- **Ask God for wisdom to live YOUR LIFE!**

---

[24] John 10:10

He will be faithful to give it to you and His Word never returns void.

DECREE: I am encompassed with God's shield of favor. He surrounds me with abundance and riches. God ornaments me, adorns me with beauty, dignity, majesty and splendor. God loves me and values me. I will ask God for wisdom to live my life to the fullest and He will give it to me. God will fulfill His Word in my life as I am faithful to believe and stand on the Word.

Daily Read: Psalms 103:4-5

Think About it: What is an area in your life that you need to see that you are crowned with dignity?

SEVEN

YOU ARE A *RULER*

> *You made them rulers over the works of your hands; you put everything under their feet (Psalm 8:6).*
>
> *God blessed them and said to them, "Be fruitful and increase in number, fill the earth and subdue it. Rule over the fish of the sea and the birds of the air and over every living creature that moves on the ground," (Genesis 1:28 NIV).*

The Hebrew definition for, 'have *dominion*' or '*rule*': *t*o rule, reign, have authority, govern, really going to rule.[25]

> *"And have redeemed us to God by your blood out of **every tribe and tongue and people and nation,** and have made us kings and priests to our God; and we shall reign on the earth." (Revelation 5: 9b-10 NIV).* In verse 9 is says, *"from every tribe and language and people and nation."*

That includes you! Every tribe means everybody! You are made to rule and reign in life.

---

[25] Strong's Concordance, Bible Hub: Search, Read, Study the Bible in Many Languages ©2004-2016 by Bible Hub.

What does that mean? What does it look like and what exactly is this telling you to do?

God has created us with the same creative power as He Himself has. He has given us the Holy Spirit that will give us the wisdom and insight we need in every situation to overcome obstacles and to come out victorious. You can overcome every situation. If you get the Word on it, walk in faith for that Word, then the Truth will come to pass.

In Mark 11:22-24 it says, "that if you tell the mountain to go jump in the lake and believe it will happen, it will."(Su's paraphrase) You need to be telling your mountain of problems to go jump in the lake and believe it will happen.

Now sometimes it feels real good to whine and get someone to feel sorry for you. But in the end you will still have your problem to deal with. Why not just suck it up, get the Word that you need to stand on, tell Satan and all his hosts where to go, bind their hands and walk out your victory like a real soldier in the winning army. You already have the victory if you choose to walk in it. It is completely your choice.

> *I keep asking that the God of our Lord Jesus Christ, the glorious Father, may give you the Spirit of wisdom and revelation, so that you may know Him better. I pray also that the eyes of your heart may be enlightened in order that you may know the hope to which He has called you, the riches of His glorious inheritance in the saints, and His incomparably great power for us who believe. That power is like the working of His mighty strength, which He exerted in Christ when He raised him from the dead and seated him at his right hand in the heavenly realms, far above all rule and*

> *authority, power and dominion, and every title that can be given, not only in the present age but also in the one to come. And God placed all things under his feet and appointed Him to be head over everything for the church, which is His body, the fullness of Him who fills everything in every way (Ephesians 1:17-23 NIV).*

We are full of Christ once we accept Him as our personal Savior. We have the living God inside of our spirit.

> *1 John 4:4 AMPC says, "Little children, you are of God [you belong to Him] and have [already] defeated and overcome them [the agents of the antichrist], because He Who lives in you is greater (mightier) than he (Satan) who is in the world.*

You, as a born again believer have been given the authority to take Satan and all his hosts out of commission in your life, in your family and in your city. Jesus has given you the power and authority to do so. He said, "*whatever you bind in heaven is bound on earth and whatever you loose in heaven is loosed on earth*".[26] You have the dominion and authority to bind evil spirits as well as call forth angels to work on your behalf.

---

[26] Matthew 16:19

DECREE: I have the living God dwelling inside of me and that is greater than anything Satan can throw at me. I have the authority to bind the enemy from my life and walk in the victory Jesus bought for me at the cross. I am a ruler in this life. I have the authority to bind Satan from my life and loose victory and God's word for me. I am made to rule and reign in this life.

Daily Read: Revelation 12:11

Think About It: What is one mountain you need to tell to jump in the lake today? Take a moment and do that now!

EIGHT

YOU CAN DO ALL THINGS

> *I can do all things through Christ who strengthens me (Philippians 4:13).*
>
> *I have strength for all things in Christ Who empowers me [I am ready for anything and equal to anything through Him Who infuses inner strength into me; I am self-sufficient in Christ's sufficiency] (Philippians 4:13 AMPC).*

The definition for strength: I fill with power, make strong, to impart ability, sharing power-ability, enable.[27]

From this definition we can see this is talking about God filling us with His power, "I fill with power". We get our strength, our power to overcome satan, from Him!

In Ephesians 6 it tells us how to be strong in the Lord; it says to put on the full armor of God.

---

[27] Strong's Concordance, Bible Hub: Search, Read, Study the Bible in Many Languages.© 2004-2016 by Bible Hub

Write Your Own Script

The definition for stand in this verse is: to set up, establish, place myself, stand still and stand ready.[28]

> *In conclusion, be strong in the Lord [be empowered through your union with Him]; draw your strength from Him [that strength which His boundless might provides]. Put on God's whole armor [the armor of a heavy-armed soldier which God supplies], that you may be able successfully to stand up against [all] the strategies and the deceits of the devil. For we are not wrestling with flesh and blood [contending only with physical opponents], but against the despotisms, against the powers, against [the master spirits who are] the world rulers of this present darkness, against the spirit forces of wickedness in the heavenly (supernatural) sphere. Therefore put on God's complete armor, that you may be able to resist and stand your ground on the evil day [of danger], and, having done all [the crisis demands], to stand firmly in your place]. Stand therefore [hold your ground], having tightened the belt of truth around your loins and having put on the breastplate of integrity and of moral rectitude and right standing with God. And having shod your feet in preparation [to face the enemy with the firm-footed stability, the promptness, and the readiness produced by the good news] of the Gospel of peace. Lift up over all the [covering] shield of saving faith, upon which you can quench all the flaming missiles of the wicked [one]. And take the helmet of salvation and the sword that the Spirit wields, which is the Word of God. Pray at*

---

[28] Strong's Concordance, Bible Hub: Search, Read, Study the Bible in Many Languages.© 2004-2016 by Bible Hub

all times (on every occasion, in every season) in the Spirit, with all [manner of] prayer and entreaty, (Ephesians 6:10-18 AMPC).

How can you do all things through Christ? The first thing that Paul tells us in Ephesians is to be empowered through your union with Jesus. The word "in" in verse 10 means; from inside of, within, in the realm of.[29] How do you have union?

You have to spend time with Him!
- **Praying**
- **Listening**
- **Worshipping**
- **Reading the Word**

Remember the Word is Jesus. You will be stronger and know fully that He has your back if you will spend time with Him daily. How can anyone have a great relationship with someone that they don't spend quality and quantity time with? Spending time with Jesus needs to be your absolute top priority if you want to be strong and be able to stand. Talk to Him, listen to Him, love Him, and let Him love you.

Second we need to understand as we walk this life out on earth we are warring against the powers of darkness, not against people. When you spend time with God, Jesus and the Holy Spirit you will be able to see clearly what spirit you are warring against and you will have the tools to defeat it.

Everyday put on the **armor**. Think through what the armor is and make sure you have it in place. Satan is out to kill, steal and destroy you. You need to think

---

[29] Strong's Concordance: Search, Read, Study the Bible in Many Languages.© 2004-2016 by Bible Hub

like a soldier everyday so you aren't surprised when he tries to come at you.

You put on the **belt of truth**. Truth means the divine truth revealed to man, the Word and the word spoken to you in the time you spend with God. Keep notes, you can use a journal or write in your Bible what God is speaking to you about a verse. Just be sure and keep track. With our busy lives what you hear at the beginning of the day may be forgotten by the end. Also you may need to go back and read it a week from now, or a month, or years. God's word is always relevant to you and you can build on the words He speaks to you over time.

Put on the **breastplate of righteousness**. The breastplate protects the heart and its emotions or desires as they bear on our decisions. The heart depicts what our capacity of moral preference is. Righteousness is given through faith in Jesus Christ to all who believe.[30] The breast-plate covers the front and the back, so you are protected coming and going. The breastplate of righteousness is put in place by faith in Jesus and His death to bring about our right standing with God, or our righteousness. As we receive His righteousness we walk in obedience to His moral preferences.

Next put on the preparation of the **gospel of peace on your feet**. This means a firm footing or readiness, preparation of the good news of the Messiah to bring towards the restoration of peace in your life and the life of others. So make sure you know the Word, the Gospel of peace. You need to know the truth so that when you hear a lie you can easily take the right path. You also can then lead others to the truth.

---

[30] Romans 3:22

Then put on the **shield of faith,** and faith comes by hearing and hearing the Word of God.[31] The shield they are talking about here is a full body shield that looks like a door. It was large enough to provide full protection from an attack, "the shield of faith" which protects the whole believer, covering their whole person in spiritual warfare.[32]

How do we put on faith?
- **We read the Word.**
- **Say the Word.**
- **Believe the Word.**

We keep hearing and hearing the Word and it changes our mind to the mind of Christ.
Now put on the **helmet of salvation**. The helmet is the "hope of salvation" in the Greek translation in this verse.[33] Know where your hope comes from and what your hope is in, Jesus dying on the cross to save you and you accepting Him and by faith believing you are saved. This is your hope!

At the beginning of Ephesians 6:10 above it says the armor of a heavy-armed soldier, which God supplies. God gives you the whole armor. It's just there for the taking. Philippians 4:13 says, *"through Christ who strengthens me",* which means that Christ empowers you and enables you to increase. Through the empowering and the ability of Christ on you will have the strength to do **ALL** things. The things you are called to do in this life. To run the race God has outfitted you to run in.

---

[31] Romans 10:17
[32] Helps Word Studies Copyright 1987, 2011, by Helps Ministries Inc.
[33] Thayer's Greek Lexicon Electronic Database. Copyright 2002, 2003, 2006, 2011 by Biblesoft, Inc.

DECREE: I can do all things through Christ Jesus empowering me and armoring me. I will defeat anything that tries to come against me and keep me from running the race that I have been called to. I choose to put on the whole armor of God and defeat the enemy. I will rise up in victory and run in full power and the wisdom of God.

Daily Read: Isaiah 55:10-11

Think about it: What is one thing that you need to defeat today?

NINE

YOU ARE AN *OVERCOMER*

> *You dear children are from God and have overcome them, because the One who is in you is greater than the one who is in the world (1 John 4:4 NIV).*

This is saying that Jesus Christ, the savior of the world is in you! When you accept Him as your savior He comes in and dwells. The Holy Spirit of God is in you. Also as you dwell with Him you are in Him. It says to stay in the vine, He is the vine. The one in the world is of course, Satan. And Jesus is greater by far!

Overcome is defined as; to conquer, prevail, victorious, to carry off the victory.
Victorious is defined as; having won the victory, triumphant, winning, champion, successful, on top of, or characterized by victory.

> *For the weapons of our warfare are not physical [weapons of flesh and blood], but they are mighty before God for the overthrow and destruction of strongholds (2 Corinthians 10:4 AMP).*

As a Christian you have the Living God dwelling inside of you. This is hard to comprehend. It is something that you come to understand only by the Spirit. The Holy Spirit will reveal this to you as you meditate on the truth in the Word of God.

> *I am the vine; you are the branches. If you remain in me and I in you, you will bear much fruit; apart from me you can do nothing. (John 15:5 NIV)*

Jesus Christ the Son of God who died for us to save us and to give us an overcoming life on this earth dwells in us! Jesus the Creator of the universe lives in us. The Spirit of the living God dwells in us! This means we have His wisdom. His overcoming power is in us. His ability to lay hands on the sick and see them recover is in us. His ability to cast out demons is in us! All we have to do to walk in these truths is to believe them, have faith in the word that tells us we do indeed have this available. We need to believe what the Holy Spirit is revealing to us.

God has given us the power to overcome this world! He meant for us to have authority all the way back in the Garden of Eden, and He has made a way for us to have it now.

We as Christians, children of the Most High God, need to quit walking around defeated and letting Satan tromp all over us. Rise up and take your rightful place as children of God and take back the authority you have! You have authority over sickness, disease, poverty, lack of any kind, and the demonic. Rise up and stand against them all with your full armor on and you will prevail.

Ephesians 6:11-17 Tells us how to overcome, by putting on the full armor of God that He has provided for us. Only as we go out fully armored are we going to overcome and walk in victory.

Decree this today and often to remind yourself you have everything it takes to overcome!

DECREE: I now shod my feet with the preparation of the gospel of peace. I bind around my feet, my path in life, and the gospel of peace. I prepare with the good news, that tells me I walk in peace, wholeness, prosperity, shalom, nothing missing, nothing broken in my life.

Above all I take the shield of faith! Which is large enough to cover my whole body, it protects me in front and back, both coming and going. Faith that is a gift of God that I choose to receive, certifying that the revelation God birthed in me will come to pass. This shield of faith will extinguish every fiery dart or plan of the enemy.

Now I put on the helmet of salvation - the salvation that Jesus bought for me on the cross. I receive it and I walk in it now!

I take up my sword, the Word of Truth, to be life to me now and those promises He has given me through the Holy Spirit.

And now as I am armored up for battle I will go out as a warrior of God - in my God given authority. Not letting Satan or his demons to take any ground in my life, or my family's life, my city, my state or my country.

I am a warrior for God and He has already won the victory! I cannot be defeated!

Daily Read: 1 John 5:4

Think About It: What is one area that you need to rise up and take authority over today?

TEN

YOU ARE A *VISIONARY*

> *Brothers and sisters, I do not consider myself yet to have taken hold of it. But one thing I do: Forgetting what is behind and straining toward what is ahead, I press on toward the goal to win the prize for which God has called me heavenward in Christ Jesus. (Philippians 3:13-14 NIV)*

Paul uses the Greek word epilanthanomai, *forgetting*: which is translated, to forget, neglect, go unnoticed, to overlook, forgotten.[34] This is written in a perfect passive, so already forgotten.[35]

The past is the past now look towards the future, don't get stuck in the past.

He used the Greek word *epekteino* which is translated; straining forward in the verse. To further define it, it is to strain after, stretch forward, intensifying extend, stretching intensely towards.

---

[34] Strong's Concordance, Bible Hub: Search, Read, Study the Bible in Many Languages. © 2004-2016 by Bible Hub
[35] Helps Word Studies Copyright 1987, 2011 by Helps Ministry Inc.

> *The purposes of a person's heart are deep waters, but one who has insight draws them out (Proverbs 20:5 NIV).*

You can discover your purpose, your passion! Ask God to show you what you are made for and He will do it!

> *I will instruct you and teach you in the way you should go; I will counsel you with my loving eye on you (Psalms 32:8 NIV).*

God knows you are full of potential and wants to help you discover that. He is available and ready to talk to you right now.

The only time you should ever look back is to see how far you have come.

When you are running a race your coach will tell you to look forward. If you look back to see how close the competition is you could fall, and you definitely will slow down. In other words, look where you are going! Look towards your future, towards what you are believing for.

Write your own script. Don't rehash the past and keep your mind on the past. God has put everything in you to be a visionary. Look forward; see the vision for your life, your family. Grab onto it and don't let go. Grab it by faith and call it into existence.

DECREE: God has put His faith and wisdom in me. He has created me with a dream and passion for my life. I choose to receive His wisdom and guidance to write my own script right now. I will not look back. I press on towards to goal of my vision for my life. I walk in the fullness of what God has created in me, and I take it by faith now! In the mighty name of Jesus.

Daily read: Jeremiah 29:10-14

Think About It: What is one passion or vision you have for your life? Are you pressing forward towards it?

ELEVEN

YOU ARE A *WARRIOR*

The Lord will give (unyielding and impenetrable) strength to His people (Psalm 29:11 Amp.).

Watch, stand fast in the faith, be brave, be strong (1 Corinthians 16:13 NKJV).

For everyone born of God overcomes the world. This is the victory that has overcome the world, even our faith (1 John 5:4 NIV).

It is God who arms me with strength, and makes my way perfect. He makes my feet like the feet of deer, and sets me on my high places. He teaches my hands to make war, so that my arms can bend a bow of bronze. You have also given me the shield of Your salvation; Your right hand has held me up, Your gentleness has made me great. You enlarged my path under me, so my feet did not slip. I have pursued my enemies and overtaken them; neither did I turn back again till they were destroyed. I have pursued my enemies and overtaken them; neither did I turn back again till they were destroyed. I have wounded them, so that they could not rise; they have fallen under my feet. For you have armed me with strength for the battle; you have

> *subdued under me those who rose up against me. You have also given me the necks of my enemies; so that I destroyed those who hated me (Psalm 18:32-40 NKJV).*

Strength translated from Greek and Hebrew in these scriptures means: fortress, power, strong, stronghold.[36]

The definition for *warrior* is: a brave or experienced soldier or fighter: a person engaged or experienced in warfare.[37]

God has given us, His kids, all the tools to be mighty warriors. We have all the tools available to us to overcome Satan and his lies and our fleshly desires. It's all in the Book, His Word!
He trains us and gives us the wisdom and strength we need to overcome and win every single battle we come up against.

We have to read the Word of God.
- **Say it out loud.**
- **Pray in the Spirit for wisdom.**
- **Follow His guidance. It's as easy as that.**

Then you will win every war, every time! Hands down, no question about it. You will always win, you always overcome. Never quit, never back down. God has won it for you; He has given you the tools, the armor and the wisdom to win every battle.

Recently I had a horrible, no good, terrible week! I was standing by faith but feeling battle weary! I held

---

[36] Strongs Concordance, Bible Hub: Search, Read, Study the Bible in Many Languages. © 2004-2016 Bible Hub.
[37] Strongs Concordance, Bible Hub: Search, Read, Study the Bible in Many Languages. © 2004-2016 Bible Hub.

to this teaching. I used my tools, put my armor on and kept fighting, asked for prayer from prayer warriors, wrestled it out in the secret place, and I am conquering. What normally would take weeks or months to overcome took me a matter of days. The Word and the Truth of the Word always works! Did all of my circumstances change that quickly? No they are still in process and I'm standing for favor in all of them! But I am filled with peace and joy and strength as I stand. That is how a warrior lives!

Decree: I am a mighty warrior! Trained for battle. God arms me with physical, mental, emotional and spiritual strength. He enables me to stand on the mountain tops. He sustains me and He stoops down to make me great. He arms me for battle and makes my enemies bow at my feet. I will overcome all my enemies.

Daily read: Put on the full armor of God every day. Ephesians 6:10-17, Psalms 91

Think About It: What war are you fighting today? Have you put the Word on it, prayer on it, and are you fully armored up?

TWELVE

YOU ARE *VICTORIOUS*

> *But thanks be to God, who gives us the victory through our Lord Jesus Christ (1 Corinthians 15:57 NIV).*
>
> *Now thanks be to God who always leads us in triumph in Christ, and through us diffuses the fragrance of His knowledge in every place (2 Corinthians 2:14 NKJV).*

The Message translation says this verse like this: *In the Messiah, in Christ, God leads us from place to place in one perpetual victory parade.* Isn't that a wonderful picture? You are in one perpetual victory parade! Praise God!

The definition of victorious is: having won a victory: having ended in victory.[38]

The definition of victory is: an act of defeating an enemy or
opponent in a battle, game or other competition. Synonyms: success, triumph, conquest, wins, favorable result, mastery, superiority: the overcoming of an enemy or antagonist.[39]

---

[38] google.com
[39] google.com

You are victorious! You win! Jesus went to the cross to win freedom for you. Freedom from sin, sickness, disease, hopelessness, fear and anything else Satan is trying to throw at you. Or lie to you about. You have the victory! Say it out loud, shout it to your enemy, Satan and his hosts are defeated!

Stand up fully armored with the belt of truth, the helmet of salvation, the shield of faith, prepare your feet with the gospel of peace, put on the breastplate of righteousness and the sword of the Spirit, which is the word of God. Armor up every day and go into the battle fully prepared.[40]

> *For the Lord your God is the one who goes with you to fight for you against your enemies to give you victory (Deuteronomy 20:4 NKJV).*
>
> *For everyone born of God overcomes the world. This is the victory that has overcome the world, even our faith (1 John 5:4 NKJV).*

With God and the faith He has given us, as a gift, we stand in that faith then we will be victorious over all of our enemies. Jesus bought the victory for us on the cross and went and took back the keys to the kingdom for us the three days He was in the grave. Now we need to stand up in that truth and take back our authority that He has given us.

---

[40] Ephesians 6:13-17

DECREE: I am always victorious. God has made me victorious over all the works of Satan. I walk in victory as I stand in faith with the word of God! I am living in a victory parade! God locks arms with me and goes with me to fight off my enemies. I always overcome and win the victory. I choose to live by faith in the word of God and not give up. I keep fighting the good fight of faith. I will not grow weary. I will run and not faint. I will prevail with God.

Daily read: 1 Samuel 17:45-47

Think About It: What is one area, (finances, relationships, attitude, addictions, etc.), **you will** become **Victorious** today? Tell someone about it!

THIRTEEEN

YOU ARE FULL OF *WISDOM*

> *If any of you lacks wisdom, you should ask God, who gives generously to all without finding fault, and it will be given to him (James 1:5 NIV).*

> *If any of you lacks wisdom [to guide him through a decision or circumstance], he is to ask of [our benevolent] God, who gives to everyone generously and without rebuke or blame, and it will be given to him (James 1:5 AMPC).*

The Greek word for *wisdom*: "sophia" is defined: wisdom, insight, skill (human and divine) intelligence. Literally, "the art of using wisdom," "affection for wisdom."[41]

> *You, through Your commandments, make me wiser than my enemies; for they are ever with me. I have more understanding than all my teachers, for Your testimonies are my meditation. I understand more than the ancients, because I keep Your precepts. I have restrained my feet from every evil way, that I may keep Your word. I have not departed from Your judgments, for You Yourself have taught me.*

---

[41] Strong's Concordance
Helps Word Studies copyright 1987, 2011 by Helps Ministries, Inc.

> How sweet are Your words to my taste, sweeter than honey to my mouth! Through Your precepts I get understanding; therefore I hate every false way (Psalms 119:98-104 NKJV).

The Hebrew word for wisdom is: chakam: to be wise, to act wisely, deal wisely, skillful, teach his wisdom. As it were the embodiment of wisdom.[42]

> Get wisdom! Get understanding! Do not forget, nor turn away from the words of my mouth. Do not forsake her, and she will preserve you; love her, and she will keep you. Wisdom is the principal thing; therefore get wisdom. And in all your getting, get understanding (Proverbs 4:5-7 NKJV).

> For "who has known the mind of the Lord that he may instruct Him?" But we have the mind of Christ (1 Corinthians 2:16 NKJV).

> That the God of our Lord Jesus Christ, the Father of glory, may give to you the spirit of wisdom and revelation in the knowledge of Him, the eyes of your understanding being enlightened; that you may know what is the hope of His calling, what are the riches of the glory of His inheritance in the saint (Ephesians 1:17-18 NKJV).

Strong's Concordance gives the same definition for knowledge in this scripture as in James 1.
The definition for knowledge is: perception, discernment, recognition, intuition.[43]

---

[42] Strong's Concordance, Bible Hub: Search, Read, Study the Bible in Many Languages. ©2004-2016 by Bible Hub
[43] Strong's Concordance, Bible Hub: Search, Read, Study the Bible in Many Languages. ©2004-2016 by Bible Hub

The definition of *wisdom* is: the quality of having experience, knowledge, and good judgement; the quality of being wise.[44]

We all need wisdom in our lives every day. We need wisdom to make life choices, to live with other people and to move in the God direction for our lives. The good news is that God said just ask Him and He will give us what we need.

In Proverbs 4 where it says to "get wisdom" and that "wisdom is the principle thing" it is saying that our pursuit of wisdom is the most important thing. We need to seek God for His wisdom and He will give it to us. As we pray in the Spirit we need to ask for interpretations so we can have God's wisdom, and **HE will faithfully** give it to us. It would be to your advantage to daily and perhaps hourly get quiet and hear what the wisdom is that God has for you.

How much wisdom do you need? To **Write Your Own Script** -- to move in the calling and purpose that God has for your life you need wisdom. To walk in peace and joy you need wisdom. To know who to minister to and when, you need wisdom. To know when to go and where to go you need wisdom.

We should not ever be making life decisions without consulting with the wisdom of God.
Get wisdom, it is the principle thing!

---

[44] google.com

Write Your Own Script

Decree: I pray that the Lord Jesus Christ, the Father of glory may give me the spirit of wisdom and revelation in the knowledge of Him. I pray, *the eyes of my understanding being enlightened; that I may know what is the hope of His calling, what are the riches of the glory of His inheritance in the saints, and what is the exceeding greatness of His power toward us who believe, according to the working of His mighty power which God worked in Christ when He raised Him from the dead and seated Him at His right hand in the heavenly places. Amen (Ephesians 1:17-19).*

Daily Read: Psalm 119:97-112

Think About It: What area do you need wisdom in today? What are you going to ask God for? Take a few minutes and really think about this! Then pray and ask God for it.

FOURTEEN

YOU ARE *JOYFUL*

> *The prospect of the righteous is joy, but the hopes of the wicked come to nothing (Proverbs 10:28 NIV).*

The word *joy* is defined *as:* delight, exceeding joy, festival, happiness, mirth, pleasure rejoicing, gladness.[45]

> *Now the God of hope fill you with all joy and peace in believing, that ye may abound in hope, through the power of the Holy Ghost (Romans 15:13 KJV).*

> *May the God of hope fill you with all joy and peace in believing [through the experience of your faith] that by the power of the Holy Spirit you will abound in hope and overflow with confidence in His promises (Romans 15:13 AMPC).*

The definition of *joyful* is: feeling, expressing, or causing great pleasure and happiness. Synonyms are: cheerful, happy, jolly, merry, sunny, lighthearted, in good spirits, bubbly, exuberant, cheery, smiling, radiant.[46]

Nehemiah gives us a clue how to walk in joy.

---

[45] NAS Exhaustive Concordance of the Bible with Hebrew-Aramaic and Greek Dictionaries Copyright 1981, 1998 by The Lockman Foundation
[46] google.com

Write Your Own Script

Nehemiah said, *"Go and enjoy choice food and sweet drinks, and send some to those who have nothing prepared. This day is holy to our Lord. Do not grieve for the joy of the Lord is your strength (Nehemiah 8:10 NIV).*

Joy comes from our relationship with Jesus. We have to stay in relationship and close communion to stay joyful. Life can throw a lot of curveballs at you and you need to be prepared for these. The Word of God tells you how to stay in joy and how to stay in relationship with Jesus at all times.

One thing we have to do is pray in the Holy Spirit and realize He is in us.

> *"May the God of hope fill you with all joy and peace in believing, so that by the power of the Holy Spirit you may abound in hope (Romans 15:13 ESV).*
>
> *"But the fruit of the Spirit is love, joy, peace, patience, kindness, goodness, faithfulness (Galatians 5:22 ESV.).*

So how do we dwell here? How do we dwell in joy? By pursuing the fruit of the Spirit. How? By dwelling with Him, taking time out of your day to get alone with Him. To pray in the Spirit, to ask Him to give you revelation on the Word you read. To ask for a filling up of the Spirit daily.

Take breaks often throughout the day to pray and ask for a fill up. *You have time to check your texts, email, Facebook, Twitter, and Instagram accounts so you definitely have time to check in with the Holy Spirit!* Ask Him for wisdom in how to deal with that difficult person. How to get your work done more efficiently. Ask Him to give you strategies for new ways of doing things better. Ask Him for creativity. He will always be there waiting with arms wide open.

You don't need hours to sit and listen -- when you are used to hearing that still small voice. You need a few moments to quiet yourself throughout the day to hear Him.

If you realize you are not joyful take a few moments and ask the Holy Spirit why. Listen and follow His leading. Ask Him to fill you with His joy.

If you are in a place where you cannot seem to get out of joylessness by yourself ask for help. Ask someone you know who is full of joy. Someone who knows how to pray in power. Someone who rightly discerns the Word of Truth. Ask them to pray with you. Take time to pray in the Spirit in your secret place and hear the Word of the Lord for your situation. God has given us all the keys; we just need to use them.

Getting wisdom from others is a great way if you are so buried in the problem you cannot see the light. But when you ask for wisdom you need to be ready to really hear what they are saying to you and walk in the wisdom they present to you. Many times to get out of their yuck, people ask for wisdom, and it is given. Then when they are asked if they have followed through on that wisdom they make every excuse.

To see breakthrough in you in your life you have to make the effort. You have to walk in the wisdom given to you. You have to be willing to change. Don't expect a magic pill; you have to put the effort in. And leave all your excuses at the door.

Make time daily to read the Word of God. First thing when you wake up say, it is going to be a great day today. I expect good things to happen today. I am filled with the joy and peace of the Lord and I will walk in His wisdom. The more proactive you are with your attitude the better your days will go. Then put a smile on your face by faith and walk in His joy!

DECREE: I am full of joy! I have the Holy Spirit inside of me and He has supplied me with the gift of joy. I choose to walk in that joy. I choose joy today, over any other feelings that may try to come up inside me. I choose to walk in the fruit of the Spirit. I make a quality decision right now to put God first place in my life and go to Him when I have needs. I will walk in the fruit of **JOY** today.

Daily Read: Romans 15:1-13

Think About It: Is there a place or person in your life, that makes walking in joy difficult? What are some things you will do before that situation comes so that you can walk in joy?

FIFTEEN

YOU ARE *PEACEFUL*

> *Let the peace of Christ rule in your hearts, since as members of one body you were called to peace (Colossians 3:15 NIV).*
>
> *But the fruit of the Spirit is love, joy, peace, forbearance, kindness, goodness, faithfulness (Galatians 5:22 NIV).*
>
> *And the peace of God, which transcends all understanding, will guard your hearts and your minds in Christ Jesus (Philippians 4:7 NIV).*
>
> *You will keep in perfect peace those whose minds are steadfast, because they trust you (Isaiah 26:3 NIV).*

The definition of *peace* as; shalom: completeness, soundness, peace, health, prosperity, wholeness.[47] The definition of *peace* is: freedom from disturbance; quiet and tranquility.[48]

Doesn't this sound amazing? How do you walk in this peace?

---

[47] NAS Exhaustive Concordance of the Bible with Hebrew-Aramaic and Greek Dictionaries Copyright 1981, 1998 by the Lockman Foundation
[48] google.com

> Colossians 3:16-17 (*Voice version*) tells us to, "*Let the word of the Anointed One richly inhabit your lives. With all wisdom teach, counsel, and instruct one another. Sing the psalms, compose hymns and songs inspired by the Spirit, and keep on singing-- sing to God from hearts full and spilling over with thankfulness. Surely, no matter what you are doing (speaking, writing, or working), do it all in the name of Jesus our Master.*

Isaiah 26 tells us whoever keeps their mind steadfast on God will walk in peace. Steadfast is defined as: to stand resolutely or dutifully firm and unwavering.[49]

If we put together the wisdom from Isaiah 26 and Colossians 3 we see that we can stay in peace when we stay in God's Word, and to stay in connection with other believers who can speak into our lives and be unwavering in our stance on God's Truth. Galatians gives us another hint, be filled up with the Holy Spirit and walk in His gifts. To walk in peace takes steadfastness but not striving, it takes surrender to God's word and wisdom. Peace will dwell in your heart as you put God, His word and heavens sounds first place. When you keep things in the right order peace will rule in your heart.

If you notice peace leaving or completely gone, go get it! Pray in the Spirit, meditate on the Word, speak the Word out of your mouth, and get together with other believers so they can speak into your life. Sit with God, worship Him and listen to what He has to say. If you are anxious you need to take action and pursue peace.

---

[49] google.com

The peace of God will rule your heart, but you have to take a stance to dwell there. You have a choice! Choose peace!

Decree: I choose to dwell in peace. I choose to allow the peace of God to rule my heart. I choose today to take a solid stance on the Word of God that says I can live in peace. I take that! I accept God's peace. I ask you Holy Spirit to teach me and to give me wisdom on how to walk in peace. I ask that you fill me up with the fruit of peace today. I choose today to put my life in the right order and to put you Jesus and Your Word and Your Spirit first place in my life. Amen.

Daily read: John 14:23-27

Think About It: What is one area you will work on this week to put in the right order so that you can walk in God's peace?

SIXTEEN

YOU ARE *BLESSED*

> *If you listen closely to the voice of the Eternal your God and carefully obey all the commands I'm giving you today, He will lift you up high above every other nation on earth. All of the following blessings will be yours--in fact, they'll chase after you--if you will listen to what He tells you (Deuteronomy 28:1-2 The Voice version).*
>
> *So do not fear, for I am with you; do not be dismayed, for I am your God. I will strengthen you and help you; I will uphold you with my righteous right hand (Isaiah 41:10 NIV).*
>
> *Blessed is the one who does not walk in step with the wicked or stand in the way that sinners take or sit in the company of mockers, but whose delight is in the law of the Lord, and who meditates on his law day and night. That person is like a tree planted by the streams of water, which yields its fruit in season and whose leaf does not wither-- whatever they do prospers (Psalm 1:1-3 NIV).*
>
> *And God is able to bless you abundantly, so that in all things at all times, having all that*

> *you need, you will abound in every good work (2 Corinthians 9:8 NIV).*

The definition for "all that you need", which is "sufficiency", the Greek word is autarkeia: defined as; self-sufficiency, which they further define as; a perfect condition of life, in which no aid or support is needed. This also is defined as contentment and competence.[50]

> *God is ready to overwhelm you with more blessings than you could ever imagine so that you'll always be taken care of in every way and you'll have more than enough to share (2 Corinthians 9:8 The Voice version).*

There are so many scriptures on God's blessings to His children. God loves you so much and wants His kids blessed! He does not ever, ever want to curse you! Satan is out to kill, steal and destroy you; God wants to bless you here and in heaven. You have to get that straight in your heart so you do not buy the lies from Satan that God is trying to teach you something through hardship or trauma. God is a good, good Father and He would and will never treat you badly! He wants you blessed so you can be blessed and so you can bless others. How can you be a blessing to others if you are barely making it yourself? He wants to bless you spiritually, physically, and emotionally.

I have had to change this old mind set myself. Satan has done a good job throughout history and through the teaching of the Church to say God wants you poor, needy, sick and broken down in spirit, to keep

---

[50] Strongs Concordance,
Thayer's Greek Lexicon, Electronic Database. Copyright 2002, 2003, 2006, 2011 by Biblesoft, Inc.

you humble and under His thumb. Many church leaders throughout history have wanted to keep their people subdued under their power, which is not God, that is just man and his pride.

God is shouting from His scripture that He wants you blessed, happy, healthy and ready to meet the needs of others.

> *And God is able to make all grace [every favor and earthly blessing] come in abundance to you, so that you may always [under all circumstances, regardless of the need] have complete sufficiency in everything [being completely self-sufficient in Him], and have an abundance for every good work and act of charity (2 Corinthians 9:8 AMPC).*

How do you change the wrong thinking that says God wants you poor and broken down, mentally, spiritually and financially? You have to put the truth of the Word in, a lot! You have to reprogram your mind to the truth of God's Word. Start with these scriptures and go hunt out all the rest of the good news in the Word. Put the Word of God in more than you put the things of the world. Do you have to do this to be saved? Nope, you can stay broke and miserable and barely making it and still make it to heaven. Will you be able to further God's kingdom while you are here on earth? Maybe, but you will have a lot better chance as a blessed child of the Most High God.

Decide today to walk in the blessing that your Father God has promised you.

Decree: God is able to make all grace, every favor and earthly blessing to come in abundance to me, today! I will have complete sufficiency in everything and be completely self-sufficient in Him. I will have abundance so that I can give on every occasion. I choose today to walk in God's prosperity, abundance, health; physically, emotionally and spiritually-- all of God's blessings. I will not walk in the counsel of the wicked (those who walk in unbelief) or follow their advice. I will delight in the law and precepts or the Word of God.

Now when you don't see your bank account fill up tomorrow, or your body healed, what are you going to do? You are going to stand by faith on the Word of God and **say,** praise God I am walking in the blessings of God. Everything I put my hand to prospers and I am able to be generous on every occasion. My body is healed in the name of Jesus through His shed blood on the cross. He already paid for it and it is my inheritance!
Then keep being generous and keep believing by faith and keep standing on the Word of God and you will have break through. You will have the blessings of God on your life, because God your Father loves you and wants to bless you and all those you can reach as well. What if you still feel depressed and low? Stand up, put a smile on your face and say my God loves me, He has chosen to bless me. I am blessed, I am happy I am full of His peace and goodness and I am able to bless others that are around me today. Keep the Word before you. Write out your scriptures, keep them with you and say them often. The Word of God is alive and active and will cut through Satan's lies faster than anything. Thankful persistence in the Word in impossible circumstances will manifest miracles for you! This

Write Your Own Script

means to thank God for the answer consistently even before you see your miracle!

Daily Read: Deuteronomy 28:1-14

Think About It: What is one area you will decide to receive your blessing this week? Do you physical healing, financial breakthrough, relationship blessing? What scriptures will you use?

SEVENTEEN

YOU ARE *RIGHTEOUS*

> *God made him who had no sin to be sin for us, so that in Him we might become the righteousness of God (2 Corinthians 5:21 NIV).*
>
> *He made Christ who knew no sin [judicially] be sin on our behalf, so that in Him we would become the righteousness of God [that is, we would be made acceptable to Him and placed in a right relationship with Him by His gracious lovingkindness] (2 Corinthians 5:21 AMPC).*

The definition of *righteousness* is: justice, righteousness of which God is the source or the author, a divine righteousness.[51]

Your righteousness has been bought and paid for by Jesus Christ. All you have to do is accept the gift and take it by faith. Matthew 5:6 shows us how to take it.

> *Blessed are those who hunger and thirst for righteousness for they shall be satisfied (Matthew 5:6 NKJV).*

---

[51] Strong's Concordance, Bible Hub: Search, Read, Study the Bible in Many Languages. © 2004-2016 Bible Hub

The Greek definition of hunger and thirst means exactly that, to be hungry and thirsty, to greatly desire that thing.[52]

The definition for satisfied or filled; is to feed, fatten, to supply in abundance.[53]

So when you seek God with all your heart He will satisfy you to the full, in abundance with His righteousness. His right standing. Not your striving to be good, but His goodness! Now am I saying you're off the hook for making right and moral choices? Nope, not at all. When you put God first and hunger and thirst for Him, guess what? You are going to want to do things that please Him and that are good for your life and other people as well. It all comes from our pursuit of Him.

> *But first and most importantly seek (aim at, strive after) His kingdom and His righteousness [His way of doing and being right--the attitude and character of God] and all these things will be given to you also (Matthew 6:33 AMP).*

The definition of "seek" is: search for, desire, require and demand.[54]

The definition of "first" is: before, at the beginning, firstly (in time, place, order, or importance) chiefly (at, at the) first of all.[55]

---

[52] Strong's Concordance, Bible Hub: Search, Read, Study the Bible in Many Languages. © 2004-2016 Bible Hub

[53] Thayer's Greek Lexicon, Electronic Database Copyright 2002,2003,2006,2011 by Biblesoft, Inc.

[54] Strong's Exhaustive Concordance, Bible Hub: Search, Read, Study the Bible in Many Languages. ©2004- 2016

[55] Strong's Exhaustive Concordance, Bible Hub: Search, Read, Study the Bible in Many Languages. ©2004- 2016

The definition for "added to you", "or will be given to you": is to properly, put together for a purpose; reaching the goal for doing it.[56]

As you seek God first and wholly go after Him, you will receive the attitude and character of God, or His righteousness. This verse is saying that as you search for, desire, require and demand God's kingdom (His way of doing things)--first, at the beginning, the very most important thing you do. It (all of these things, whatever it is you need in life), will be given to you properly put together in the exact way that you need it.

Now most people have the excuse of, "I don't have enough time", or "you really don't understand, I'm working two jobs and going to school" or I have kids, or a myriad of other excuses. First of all if you will seek God first you will have more time. God will help you with strategies to get things done quicker and more efficiently. He will give you one job that meets all your needs and leaves you time. Honestly most people have time to read the Word and pray at least a half hour a day. Most people spend that much on social media or in front of the television every day.

Some other creative ways to get more word time or prayer time in is to listen to teachings in the car or the Bible being read. Or you can use this time to pray. Your workout time can be used to listen to teaching or scripture being read. While making dinner you can be listening to teachings or the word being read, or worship music. During your shower time you can be praying instead of worrying. While getting ready for the day listen to teaching. If you start asking the Holy Spirit to show you time in your

---

[56] Helps Word Studies copyright 1987, 2011 by Helps Ministries, Inc.

day to pursue your relationship with Jesus and therefore His righteousness, He will give you the insight you need.

Decree: I will make it a priority in my heart to pursue You and to be filled with Your righteousness. Create in me the desire to make You first place in my life Lord, and I will take the steps to do it. Show me the value of putting my relationship with You first in my life. I will choose to realize You only have my good in mind and in our relationship. You will always bless me abundantly, and I choose today to receive it. Thank you for Your gift of righteousness that I could never fulfill by myself. Thank you for loving me so completely, I choose to walk in the righteousness!

Daily Read: Psalms 92:12-15

Think About It: What is one time waster you can deal with today?

EIGHTEEN

YOU ARE *COURAGEOUS*

> "Be strong and courageous, do not be afraid or tremble in the dread before them, for it is the Lord your God who goes with you. He will not fail you or abandon you." Then Moses called to Joshua and said to him in the sight of all [the people of] Israel, "Be strong and courageous, for you will go with this people into the land which the Lord has sworn to their fathers to give them, and you will give it to them as an inheritance. It is the Lord who goes before you; He will be with you. He will not fail you or abandon you. Do not fear or be dismayed" (Deuteronomy 31: 6-8 AMP).

I want to start off by telling you a little clue in how to study and absorb the Bible. The whole Bible is for YOU, right now, in this life. The Old Testament is testimonies of God's care of His people, prophetic words that are still coming true today and specific words for your situation. As God is talking to Joshua here in this passage, He is saying the same thing to you today. Be strong and courageous! Then He tells us how to do it. It's God with you. You staying in communion and conversation with Him to know your next move. He will guide you.

The Hebrew definition for *courage* is: to make strong, mighty, stronger, steadfastly minded, fortify, establish, prevail, to be alert, establish.[57]

The definition of courageous is: not deterred by danger or pain; brave. Synonyms include; brave, fearless, valiant, heroic, lionhearted, bold, daring, undaunted, unflinching, unafraid, indomitable, and gallant.[58] These are strong words!

> *"You see; God did not give us a cowardly spirit but a powerful, loving, and disciplined spirit (2 Timothy 1:7).*

The word "powerful" in this word comes from the word "dunamis" and it means; miraculous power, might and strength.[59]

God has given us this as a gift. We just have to accept it and walk in it. I know this isn't as easy as it sounds on this page. It's not easy, but it is simple. It's as simple as putting in the Word of God and standing on it and not what you see.

Joshua was taking over a land that had actual giants in it. **But God said**! You need to remember these 3 words. But God said you are healed! But God said you will prosper! But God said you will fulfill the destiny for your life. These are basic words for everyone out there. But what has God said personally to you? Are you standing on it or being lied to by the enemy of your life?

---

[57] Strong's Exhaustive Concordance, Bible Hub: Search, Read, Study the Bible in Many Languages.© 2004- 2016 by Bible Hub
[58] Google.com
[59] Strong's Exhaustive Concordance, Bible Hub: Search, Read, Study the Bible in Many Languages.© 2004- 2016 by Bible Hub

I have 8 kids, each of my children has had a life threatening situation at their birth, but now they are all strong and mighty and going for God! Satan knew that the day they were born and he is out to kill, steal and destroy. So when these situations came up surrounding them, I would either stomp my foot in reality or in my mind and say NO! God said they will live and not die![60] I will be blessed with children![61] This child is a gift from God and He gives only perfect gifts and He does not change![62]

I had many more verses that I stood on for my children. I also knew who my God was! He is a loving kind God who is not out to hurt me or my children. Because I have studied and meditated on these truths, and my husband and I have stood firmly in our faith, all of my children are here, in great health and following God.

How do you walk in courage? You get the Word on it. You meditate on it until it becomes a part of you. You know it so well that when a circumstance comes up that is against the Word you know you will stand up, steadfastly and courageously say NO! This is not true! I know what the Word says about this, I know who my God is and I know who I am! Satan you cannot lie to me, I know the truth.

> *Have I not commanded you? Be strong and courageous! Do not be terrified or dismayed (intimidated), for the Lord your God is with you wherever you go (Joshua 1:9 AMP).*
>
> *Be on guard; stand firm in your faith [in God, respecting His precepts and keeping your*

---

[60] Psalms 118:17
[61] Deuteronomy 28:4
[62] James 1:7

doctrine sound]. Act like [mature] men/women and be courageous; be strong (2 Corinthians 16:13 AMP.).

DECREE: I will be courageous! I will meditate and believe the Word of God. I will believe what the Word says about me and my circumstance. I will not be moved by Satan or his lies. I choose to go with God. BUT MY GOD! He will save me; He will deliver me from the hands of the enemy! He will never leave me or forsake me. He is my tower of strength in all circumstances. I will prevail with God on my side. I will be a courageous warrior and fight the good fight of faith. I will win!

Daily Read: Deuteronomy 28:1-14

Think About It: What area in your life do you need to put courage on today? What giant will you topple today?

NINETEEN

YOU ARE *STRONG*

> *I can do all this through Him who gives me strength (Philippians 4:13 NIV).*
> *Finally, be strong in the Lord and in His mighty power (Ephesians 6:10 NIV).*
>
> *But those who hope in the Lord will renew their strength. They will run and not grow weary, they will walk and not be faint (Isaiah 40:31 NIV).*

The definition for *strong* as: enable, increase in, strength, empower, be or make strong.[63]
The dictionary definition of *strong* is: able to withstand great force or pressure. Some synonyms of strong are: powerful, long-lasting, impregnable, secure, and powerfully built.[64]

God has given you His strength, (empowered you, enabled you), to live an overcoming life on this earth. In the book of Nehemiah it says, "the joy of the Lord is our strength." As you walk in joy and **do not** let Satan steal your joy you will remain strong,

---

[63] Strong's Concordance, Bible Hub: Search, Read, Study the Bible in Many Languages. © 2004- 2016 by Bible Hub
[64] Google.com

(powerful, secure, and long-lasting). Satan has no power against **JOY!** It says that Abraham did not doubt or waver in unbelief concerning the promise of God, but he grew strong and empowered by faith, in God's promises.

Take these scriptures and meditate on them, then stand on them by faith. To stand means, able to withstand great force or pressure, indestructible, well protected, well-fortified.[65] This is how you stand strong! God has given you the key to walk in strength in your physical body, your spirit, and your emotions.

You are getting stronger and stronger every day! Say that! Decree it out loud!

Ephesians 6 tells us to draw our strength from His strength. Every believer has the ability to walk by faith in a greater place of supernatural strength that enables you to overcome anything. As you build yourself up in faith, by spending time in prayer, the Word and being filled with the Holy Spirit you are more able to overcome and resist the devil. You have to be proactive. You cannot wait until disaster strikes and then try to strengthen yourself in the Word. Start today, meditate on the Word today! Build up your strength today.

God's Word is food to your spirit. It contains all the nutrients you need to build a strong spirit. In order to grow stronger you must feed on the Word of God every day. As we meditate on it and consume it every day we will know the Truth and be able to quench all the fiery darts of Satan and stand strong! You will be able to recognize the lies of this world and the enemy and stay strong when they try to come against you.

---

[65] Google.com

He is my strength, and He is the reason I sing; He has been there to save me in every situation (Psalms 118:14 The Voice version).

With a strong spirit you will be able to overcome any financial problems, relationship problems, spiritual issues, physical weaknesses and everything the devil throws at you and you will walk in peace and know you are strong.

When you spend time in the Word of God and worshipping God you are grounding your spirit to the Truth of God. You will be strong to repel disease, resist sin, override doubt, and walk in forgiveness. We can build up our strength in God and His Word to such a degree that sickness can't affect us, fear can't stop us, and bad news will not move us.

DECREE: I am strong in the Lord. I draw strength from the Lord and His truths. My strong spirit, that is rooted in the Word of God, will sustain me in bodily pain or trouble. The Lord is my strength and I will run and not grow weary! I will walk in strength and the truth of God's word and be steadfast as my rock foundation. I will overcome all attacks from the enemy. I will win!

DAILY READ: Psalms 91

Think About It: Do you think you have a strong spirit? If not what are you going to do about that today?

TWENTY

YOU ARE *FAITHFUL*

> But My righteous one [the one justified by faith] shall live by faith [respecting man's relationship to God and trusting Him] (Hebrews 10:38 Amp.).

> For everyone born of God is victorious and overcomes the world; and this is the victory that has conquered and overcome the world-- our [continuing, persistent] faith [in Jesus the Son of God] (1 John 5:4 Amp.).

The Greek definition of *faith* is: faithfulness, belief, trust, confidence.[66]
The definition of *faithful* is: constant, loyal, true, devotion, steadfast, qualities of stability.[67]

If you are a born again believer in Jesus Christ and have accepted Him as your personal Savior you are faithful, (full of faith). Faith is a gift from God and never generated by us. However we need to accept His gift and walk in it. Romans 12:3b says, "in accordance with the faith God has distributed to each of you". God gives each of us faith! He gives you faith, you just need accept it!

---

[66] Strong's Concordance
[67] Google.com

You will not have use of a gift unless you take it and unwrap it. Someone could buy you a gift, wrap it up all nice and give it to you, but if you leave it on the counter and never unwrap it you will not receive the gift, it will not be a value to you.

Faith comes as Christ speaks His Word to your spirit, through the Word and through the Holy Spirit.

> *Consequently, faith comes from hearing the message, and the message is heard through the word about Christ (Romans 10:17 NIV).*

We are all gifted a portion of faith when we accept Jesus as our Savior. But to grow in faith we need to read and study the Word and ask the Holy Spirit to fill us up, to grow our faith. The word hearing in Romans 10:17 means hearing and hearing and keep on hearing. Continually hearing the Word will bring growing, mature faith. It is our gift from God, but we have to unwrap it!

Faith is not natural it is spiritual, a gift from God. You cannot command faith to come or will it to come. You receive it as a gift and build up your faith by hearing God's word. We are faithful only because God has gifted it to us. As we receive His gift and stay in His Word so that He can build our faith we will be faith-FULL.

> *For it is by grace you have been saved, through faith--and this is not from yourselves, it is the gift of God---not by works, so that no one can boast (Ephesians 2:8-9 NIV).*

Reading the Word, spending time with Jesus, worshipping Him, and spending time receiving all the Holy Spirit has to give you is not "works"! Religious duty is works. Don't get those mixed up. Pleasing man is works, doing things to bring attention from man is, but pleasing God is not.

So receive your gift from God, dwell in His word and get built up in His most holy faith.

DECREE: I receive God's gift of faith right now, today. I choose today to un-wrap His gift, the Word of God and to be built up in His most Holy faith. I will hear and keep hearing the Word of God. I choose this day to walk in the gift of faith. I choose this day to do the work that it takes to put in the Word of God in my life.

Daily Read: Hebrews 10:19-29

Think About It: Decide on one way you will put more Word in this week.

TWENTY-ONE

YOU ARE *SIGNIFICANT*

> *Look, if you sold a few sparrows, how much money would you get? A copper coin apiece, perhaps? And yet your Father in heaven knows when those small sparrows fall to the ground. You beloved, are worth so much more than a whole flock of sparrows. God knows everything about you, even the number of hairs on your head. So do not fear! (Matthew 10:29-31 The Voice version).*

> *Then God said, "Let us make mankind in our image, in our likeness, so that they may rule over the fish in the sea and the birds in the sky, over the livestock and all the wild animals, and over all the creatures that move along the ground." So God created mankind in His own image, in the image of God He created them; male and female He created them (Genesis 1:26-27 NIV).*

You are significant! God created you in His image! You are designed like God is. He didn't make animals like himself only humans. Not only did He create us in His very own image but He breathed His breath into us. His very life, His Spirit.

God always knows where you are, He sees you. You are significant. Now this can be frightening for someone living in sin and trying to hide. But for His children it is very comforting.

The definition of *significant i*s: remarkable, worthy of attention; noteworthy. Synonyms are: extraordinary, exceptional, amazing, astounding, marvelous, wonderful, stunning, and incredible.[68] The list goes on!

God thinks you are significant! He also thinks you are extraordinary, exceptional, amazing, astounding, marvelous, wonderful, stunning and incredible! He's your Dad and He loves you and sees only the potential in you. Sometimes our earthly dad's don't do this for us, but God, our Father always does.

You are the temple of the Holy Spirit, He dwells in you and empowers you to heal the sick, cast out demons and preach the gospel.

> *Do you not know that you are God's temple and that God's Spirit lives in you? If someone destroys God's temple, God will destroy him. For God's temple is holy, which is what you are (1 Corinthians 3:16-17 ESV).*

Wow! You are the temple of God and you are holy! Through Jesus Christ and his sacrifice at Calvary we have been made the temple of God and made holy. You are significant!

---

[68] Google.com

DECREE: I am raised up with Jesus and empowered to walk in freedom and power on this earth. I am significant! God the Father and Jesus the Son see me as significant! I am empowered to do the works that You did while on the earth. I am loved by Jesus enough that He chose to die for me to buy my redemption. I am seen by God and my life is significant!

Daily read: Psalms 23

Think About It: Take one of the synonyms: extraordinary, exceptional, amazing, astounding, marvelous, wonderful, stunning, or incredible, now think about the fact that this describes you in the sight of God! The creator of the universe.

TWENTY TWO

YOU ARE *FREE*

> Now the Lord is the Spirit, and where the Spirit of the Lord is, there is liberty [emancipation from bondage, true freedom] (2 Corinthians 3:17 Amp.).
>
> *Now the Lord is the Spirit, and where the Spirit of the Lord is, there is freedom (2 Corinthians 3:17 NIV).*

Guess where the Spirit of the Lord is?

> *By this we know that we abide in Him and He in us, because He has given us of His Spirit. And we have seen and testify that the Father has sent the Son as Savior of the world. Whoever confesses that Jesus is the Son of God, God abides in him, and he in God (1 John 4:13-15 NKJV).*
>
> Do you not know that you are a temple of God and that the Spirit of God dwells in you (1 Corinthians 3:16 NKJV)?

He, Jesus is in us. 2 Corinthians 3:17 says, *"where the Spirit of the Lord is there is freedom."* Therefore there is freedom in us by the indwelling of the Holy Spirit. Feel free to get up and dance!

The definition for freedom or liberty is: a state of freedom from slavery.[69]

You are free from slavery to sin and death. You are free from bondages and all the evil that Satan has brought to this earth. You are free now! Not just when you get to heaven.

In the worldly perspective freedom means the right to do whatever you want to do. It means doing your own thing without thought to the feelings or effect on others. It is the right to your own personal choice, regardless of the outcome to others. This type of freedom actually results in slavery and bondage to sin and death.

The kind of freedom that these verses are talking about is freedom to choose God and His ways over sin. The freedom from Satan and his lies over your life. It means freedom to walk in divine health instead of sickness, to walk in Godly prosperity instead of poverty and lack. To walk in hope and to be able to live out your destiny. It means freedom from generational curses and old habits. It is freedom to not worry about yourself because you know God, your Father loves you and will take care of you as you love and focus on others. It means freedom from the curse of the law and walking in the salvation Jesus bought for us on the cross. This is true freedom.

---

[69] Strong's Concordance, Bible Hub: Search, Read, Study the Bible in Many Languages. ©2004-2016 by Bible Hub.

DECREE: I choose to accept Jesus as my personal Savior and receive the freedom He bought for me on the cross. I choose to walk in freedom today from the curse of the law, from selfishness and from sin. I will choose love today. I walk in freedom from the curse, from sickness, disease, depression, hopelessness, worry, lack and death of any kind. I walk with the Holy Spirit and in the freedom and liberty of Christ.

Daily read: Galatians 5

Think About It: What is one bondage in your life? Jesus has already set you free from this! Will you choose to walk in freedom in this area today?

TWENTY-THREE

YOU ARE *UNOFFENDABLE*

> When He was verbally abused, He didn't return the abuse; when He suffered, He didn't make threats to cause suffering in return; instead, He trusted that all would be put right by the one who is just when He judges (1 Peter 2:23 The Voice version).

> Banish bitterness, rage and anger, shouting and slander, and any and all malicious thoughts--these are poison. Instead, be kind and compassionate. Graciously forgive one another just as God has forgiven you through the Anointed, our Liberating King (Ephesians 4:31-32 The Voice version).

The definition of *unoffendable i*s: Incapable of being offended; unlikely to take offence.[70]

How did Jesus remain unoffendable? He trusted that God had His back and that He could absolutely take care of Him and bring good out of every circumstance and situation in His life.

Am I saying you should stay in an abusive relationship? No way! Get out now! But I am saying that when someone hurts you to trust that God can

---

[70] Oxford Dictionaries.com Oxford University Press copyright 2017

take care of you and bring good to you. That He has your back and even when someone tries to harm you, God will bring good to you through it, He will turn the tables over and make the situation become a blessing to you.

Recently a ministry posted a short piece on a social media account. It very quickly went viral, from the opposing side! It went viral from the people putting down what they were saying and making fun of it. Guess what 1000's of people read about Jesus and His love. Now they could of got offended about these people making fun of them and trashing what they wrote but instead they chose to thank God and believe He would work it for good, and it totally did!

I have been offended and hurt badly by people! I have had to learn to forgive and I am getting quicker at forgiving. The quicker you forgive, the quicker it brings you healing and peace so that you can move forward. I'm not saying that there isn't a process, there is!

> Not that I have already obtained it [this goal of being Christ like] or have already been made perfect, but I actively press on so that I may take hold of that [perfection] for which Christ Jesus took hold of me and made me His own (Philippians 3:12 Amp.).

Paul states that he hasn't made it all the way but he keeps pressing forward to the goal.

In order to press forward you have to choose to believe and speak out who God says you are. He says you are becoming Christ like, and He was unoffendable. When you forgive someone it does not let them off the hook, it just takes them off your hook and puts them on God's. He will take care of it, that's what you have to trust.

Instead we keep pressing ahead, and we keep working on it. Never give up or beat yourself up. Just keep swimming! You won't lose the race unless you stop! If you have someone in your life that you have been offended by forgive, then tomorrow when you wake up forgive them again. Keep doing this until the offense, or *that thing, that feeling,* isn't there anymore!

DECREE: I choose to remain unoffendable! I choose to walk in forgiveness trusting that God has this! He will bring favor and goodness to me in every situation. He will take care of those offending me. I trust Him to have my back! I choose to trust God and let go of the hurt today!

DAILY READ: Philippians 3:12-21

Think About It: What is one area you want to move forward in in your life? Think about on purpose taking that offense off your hook and putting it God's today.

Write Your Own Script

TWENTY-FOUR

YOU ARE *HOLY*

> *For He chose us in Him before the creation of the world to be holy and blameless in his sight. In love he predestined us to be adopted as His sons through Jesus Christ, in accordance with His pleasure and will -- to the praise of His glorious grace, which he has freely given us in the One he loves (Ephesians 1:4-6 NIV).*
>
> *But like the Holy One who called you, be holy yourselves also in all your behavior, because it is written, "You shall be holy, for I am holy" (1 Peter 1:15-16 ESV).*

The definition of holy is: "likeness of nature with the Lord," because "different from the world." "Set apart" and therefore different (distinguished/distinct)".[71]

Synonyms of holy: sacred, consecrated, sanctified, religious, blessed, dedicated.[72]

---

[71] Helps Word Studies copyright 1987, 2011, by Helps Ministries, Inc.
[72] Google.com

God chose us in Him to be holy, sanctified, blessed, dedicated to have connection with God and possess a certain distinction. Our body is His temple.[73]

I think many times when we hear that we are holy, or immediate response is, definitely NOT! Often this is because we think of Jesus being "without sin". As you can see as children of God, we are holy, set apart, and connected to God, a sacred place not to be profaned.

What does that last part mean? "A sacred place not to be profaned"? Our bodies are the temple of the Holy Spirit, just like in the Old Testament when the ark of the covenant that held God's glory was holy and sacred, our bodies are too. Who is told to keep our bodies holy? We are! Keeping your body holy is making morally right decisions. I know this is super unpopular right now and totally not politically correct, but yes it is necessary and possible! Choose to keep your body pure and holy, set apart for God's use. Do what is morally right, choose not to sin. What if you have already sinned? Just ask for forgiveness and He is faithful to forgive you. Then turn and go the other way and sin no more!

Is walking morally right this easy? Yes it really is. As you stay in the Word and make prayer and worship a priority each day this will be a breeze. As you build your relationship with Jesus you will want to please Him.

You are set apart in God's eyes and heart to be used by Him to bring love and hope to the world.

---

[73] 1 Corinthians 6:19

DECREE: I am set apart for God's use, to bring the message of love and peace to this world. I will choose to walk in purity and make moral decisions to live my life. I choose to walk set apart for His purposes, sanctified and blessed. I will be dedicated to God, His Word and His ways for my life.

Daily Read: 1 Peter 2:9

Think About It: Do you see yourself as holy and set apart for God's use?

TWENTY-FIVE

YOU ARE LOVED

> *That Christ may dwell in your hearts through faith; that you, being rooted and grounded in love, may be able to comprehend with all the saints what is the width and length and depth and height--to know the love of Christ which passes knowledge; that you may be filled with all the fullness of God. Now to Him who is able to do exceedingly abundantly above all that we ask or think, according to the power that works in us, to Him be glory in the church by Christ Jesus to all generations, forever and ever. Amen (Ephesians 3:17-21 NKJV).*

The Greek definition for *love:* love, goodwill, esteem.[74]
Synonyms for goodwill: compassion, goodness, kindness, sympathy, understanding.[75]
Synonyms for esteem: respect, admiration, favor, recognition.[76]

To know the love, (goodness, kindness, sympathy, understanding, respect, admiration, favor and recognition) of Christ which passes knowledge.

---

[74] Strong's Concordance, Bible Hub: Search, Read, Study the Bible in Many Languages. © 2004-2016 by Bible Hub
[75] Google.com
[76] Google.com

That's what this scripture is saying! I can hear the naysayers now. God doesn't respect us; we are supposed to respect Him only. God doesn't admire us, we are lowly sinners! Read that scripture again. Think about how God sent His own Son to die for us to save us. Meditate on all the scriptures where God says He blesses you and favors you. If we Christians, God's children could comprehend even a small portion of God's love for us it would not only change our lives but those around us!

Jesus loves you! Father God loves you! They love you so much that they want to do everything they can to convey that love to you. God sent the Holy Spirit to fill you up with the knowledge of His love. You can know the fullness of His love by spending time dwelling in His presence and inviting the Holy Spirit in. This is important. Trying to comprehend God's love from others telling you will only go so far. When you bask in the presence of God with the filling up of the Holy Spirit you will truly comprehend the love of your heavenly Father and your Savior.

Some of us didn't have a great father figure to fully understand "father love". If this applies to you I suggest you really push into the secret place with God and let Him wash you free from your preconceived concept of a father's love. I have had to do this and I can tell you it works! One thing I am sure of is how much my Father God loves me!

> *In this the love of God was made manifest among us, that God sent his only Son into the world, so that we might live through him. In this is love, not that we have loved God but that he loved us and sent his Son to be the propitiation for our sins. Beloved, if God so loved us, we also ought to love one another (1 John 4:9-11 NKJV).*

God loved you so much that He sent His Son to die for your salvation to bring you back into right standing with Him. God loves you! Say that to yourself until you believe it! God's love for you is not dependent on your performance; it's dependent on God's gift.

DECREE: God loves me so much! He thinks about me and every detail of my life, every day, every moment. He loves me so much He wants to be involved in all of the details of my life. I will spend time sitting with God today and leaning into Him in order to realize how much He loves me.

Daily Read: Psalms 136

Think About It: Pick one of the synonyms: compassion, goodness, kindness, sympathy, understanding, respect, admiration, favor, recognition. Now meditate on how God sees you through this lens.

TWENTY- SIX

YOU ARE FILLED WITH *GRACE*

> *Yet grace (God's unmerited favor) was given to each of us individually [not discriminately, but in different ways] in proportion to the measure of Christ's [rich and bounteous] gift (Ephesians 4:7 AMPC.).*
>
> *May grace (God's favor) and peace (which is perfect wellbeing, all necessary good, all spiritual prosperity, and freedom from fears and agitating passions and moral conflicts) be multiplied to you in [the full, personal, precise, and correct] knowledge of God and of Jesus our Lord (2 Peter 1:2 AMPC).*

The Greek definition of *grace*: a gift or blessing brought to man by Jesus, favor, kindness.[77]

The definition of grace is: the free and unmerited favor of God, as manifested in salvation of sinners and the bestowal of blessings.[78]

Of course there is the definition of being physically graceful, but that is not what we are talking about here.

---

[77] Strong's Concordance, Bible Hub: Search, Read, Study the Bible in Many Languages. © 2004 - 2016 by Bible Hub
[78] Google.com

My name means grace, but in my mind I'm definitely do not think of myself as graceful! I'm loud and aggressive and passionate, the opposite of what I think of as grace, which is, quiet, sweet, nonobtrusive! But that is not what my name means or what the Word is saying here. Grace is believing, and walking in the unmerited favor of God! Again we have to un-wrap the gift to be able to receive the benefit of it.

In 2 Peter it is talking about God's favor that he bestows on us, puts on us.

Synonyms of favor are: approval, goodwill, kindness, backing, support, assistance.[79] God's got your back!

We have taught our children and ourselves to believe we are walking in the favor of God, which is the grace of God. When a good thing happens, when we get the best job or a really good deal on a purchase, or the front parking spot, we say that's the favor of God on our life. That's God's grace towards you.

God wants to be of assistance to you every day, even in the little things. Look for His favor in your life. Thank Him for His support and backing in your life. Start taking note of the grace/favor of God on your life.

---

[79] Google.com

DECREE: Father God, thank you for your unmerited grace/favor pouring over my life. I am blessed beyond measure; above all I can dare ask or think. I freely receive God's grace/favor in my life. I choose to un-wrap the gift of grace you freely want to give me. I will spend time with the Holy Spirit so that He can make me aware of God's favor in my life today!

Daily Read: Ephesians 4:7-12

Think About It: What is one area in your life where you will choose to see God's grace applied? Is it your job, relationships, health, emotions? Apply His grace, favor, assistance, kindness, support, backing, approval, goodwill.

TWENTY-SEVEN

YOU ARE *ROYAL HEIRS:*

> *And if we are [His] children, then we are [His] heirs also: heirs of God and fellow heirs with Christ [sharing His inheritance with Him]; only we must share His suffering if we are to share His glory (Romans 8:17 AMPC).*

The moment you are saved you become heirs to the "Royal family" that owns and operates the entire universe. You received an inheritance so vast; it will take all of eternity to fully comprehend it.[80]

The definition of heir is: "someone who has been appointed to receive an inheritance."[81] An heir receives something of value from someone.

> *Galatians 4:7 AMPC says, "Therefore, you are no longer a slave (bond servant) but a son; and if a son, then [it follows that you are] an heir by the aid of God, through Christ.*

> *But you are a chosen race, a royal priesthood, a dedicated nation, [God's] own purchased, special people, that you may set forth the wonderful deeds and display the virtues and*

---

[80] Ephesians 2:7
[81] Gotquestions.org Copyright 2002-2016 Got Questions Ministries

perfections of Him Who called you out of darkness into His marvelous light (1 Peter 2:9 AMPC).

You are an heir to God's kingdom so you can spread His goodness throughout the world. You have access to all that is His. He will support you and bless you so that you can be a blessing to this world. The world around you needs you to fully comprehend that you are God the Father's heir, joint heir with Jesus Christ and you are here to bring the love, joy, peace, and healing that Jesus brought when He was on the earth.

You have inherited God's attributes, as His child. You also inherit His authority in this earth! You are no longer a slave! You are no longer a slave to sin, sickness, hopelessness, lack or death of any kind. You are an heir of the most High God! Read the Book, (the Bible) and see what your family owns.

DECREE: I am a joint heir of the Royal Priesthood of God. I share Jesus' inheritance with Him! I choose today to walk in my inheritance as someone special, set apart and holy. Thank you for blessing me and valuing me! I will walk in that knowledge today! I choose today to walk in my inheritance and take authority over sin, death and lack in any area in my life.

Daily Read: Colossians 1:2, Titus 3:7

Think About It: How would walking in your inheritance change your life? How could you minister God's love more effectively if you fully understood your inheritance?

TWENTY-EIGHT

YOU ARE *CHOSEN*

> *But you are a chosen race, a royal priesthood, a dedicated nation, [God's] own purchased, special people, that you may set forth the wonderful deeds and display the virtues and perfections of Him Who called you out of darkness into His marvelous light (1 Peter 2:9 AMPC).*

> *But this is not you, dearly beloved brothers and sisters of the Lord. We cannot help but thank God for you at all times because from the beginning He handpicked you for salvation through the Spirit's sanctifying work and your belief in the truth (2 Thessalonians 2:13 The Voice version).*

The Greek definition for chosen is: to select, choose, selected, especially as a deeply personal choice- literally "chosen, out of a personal preference."[82]

The definition of *chosen* is: having been selected as the best or most appropriate. Synonyms for chosen is: selected, appointed, elected, favored, and handpicked.[83]

---

[82] Helps Word-studies ©1987, 2011 by Helps Ministries, Inc.
[83] Google.com

Write Your Own Script

Have you ever wanted to be the one that was picked from a deeply personal choice? That was favored and selected especially for that specific circumstance? I think most of us feel that on a daily basis! I know for me when I was a mom of babies it felt so good to be their first choice always! It really feels good.

God the Father chose each one of us. God selected us as the best, most appropriate person. He handpicked us to love. He also bestows His favor on us. He did this by sending His only Son to die for us which brings us redemption. He didn't just choose a few, He chose all of mankind. But He gave us the freedom of choice to choose Him. He already picked you! He did everything necessary to make it possible for you to come into right relationship with Him. He fixed what Adam and Eve screwed up. He paid the price to buy us back from slavery to Satan. He paid the full price; there is nothing left that we owe! All you have to do is say yes to His favor, His love, His freedom, His peace, (nothing missing, nothing broken), His health and wholeness, and His prosperity on this earth. Everything that the blood of Jesus bought for us on the cross. Jesus chose you! He sacrificed His life for you, so that you could walk in the appointed favor, a sure election of right standing and handpicked for the love of the Father. He chose you; all He is waiting for to move in your life is for you to choose Him!

If you have not asked Jesus into your heart all you have to do is say, YES! Yes I believe Jesus, yes I choose you!

> *For God so greatly loved and dearly prized the world that He [even] gave up His only begotten (unique) Son, so that whoever believes in (trusts in, clings to, relies on) Him shall not*

perish (come to destruction, be lost) but have eternal (everlasting) life (John 3:16 AMPC).

Choose Him! He has already chosen you and loves you so much!

DECREE: Jesus I choose you, today and I will choose you tomorrow! I am a chosen one dearly and deeply loved by God the Father and Jesus the Son! I love you Lord and accept you as my personal Lord and Savior over every single aspect of my life. I CHOOSE YOU JESUS! I choose to walk in the fullness of everything you paid for at Calvary. I will walk as a chosen one and walk in the light of God's love.

Daily read: 2 Thessalonians 2:13-15

Think About It: Think about how much Jesus loves you today! How He chose you before you chose Him.

DECREES

ONE: YOU ARE GOD'S WORKMANSHIP:

DECREE: I am God's workmanship; I am created by God, the Creator of the universe! I operate from the Holy Spirit; I have the mind of Christ and walk in His truth. I am enough, I am worthy, and I will reach my goals!

TWO: YOU HAVE THE *MIND* OF CHRIST:

DECREE: I have the mind of Christ. I have the wisdom of God, which He freely gives to me as His beloved child. I will put in the Word, which is Christ and renew my mind daily to walk in His truth and wisdom. I hear the voice of the Lord and will incline my ear to His voice. I choose to walk with the Spirit of God.

THREE: YOU HAVE A NEW *IMAGE:*

DECREE: I am being ever transformed in the knowledge of Christ. I am being created in the image of God from glory to glory by the Spirit of the Lord. As I renew my mind to understand who I am in Christ, I will be changed into God's image on the inside and outside as well.

FOUR: YOU ARE *FEARFULLY, WONDERFULLY* MADE AND *MARVELOUS:*

DECREE: I am fearfully made. I inspire reverence to God everywhere I go. I am distinguished, set apart, for Your kingdom, Lord. I am marvelously and extraordinarily made! I am God's workmanship, created in His exact image. He created me with a passion to fulfill a purpose on the earth. I believe this! I choose this day to walk in this truth.

FIVE: YOU ARE MORE THAN A *CONQUEROR*

DECREE: I am a conqueror through Jesus my Lord. I prevail mightily and am overwhelmingly victorious. I will prevail completely over every problem and enemy in my life. Thank you, God for always giving me the victory. I will build up my faith with the Word and praying in the Spirit today.

SIX: YOU ARE CROWNED WITH *GLORY* AND *HONOR*

DECREE: I am encompassed with God's shield of favor. He surrounds me with abundance and riches. God ornaments me, adorns me with beauty, dignity, majesty and splendor. God loves me and values me. I will ask God for wisdom to live my life to the fullest and He will give it to me. God will fulfill His Word in my life as I am faithful to believe and stand on the Word.

SEVEN: YOU ARE A *RULER*

DECREE: I have the living God dwelling inside of me and that is greater than anything Satan can throw at me. I have the authority to bind the enemy from my life and walk in the victory Jesus bought for me at the cross. I am a ruler in this life. I have the authority to bind Satan from my life and loose victory and God's word for me. I am made to rule and reign in this life.

EIGHT: YOU CAN DO ALL THINGS

DECREE: I can do all things through Christ Jesus empowering me and armoring me. I will defeat anything that tries to come against me and keep me from running the race that I have been called to. I choose to put on the whole armor of God and defeat the enemy. I will rise up in victory and run in full power and the wisdom of God.

NINE: YOU ARE AN *OVERCOMER*

DECREE: I now shod my feet with the preparation of the gospel of peace. I bind around my feet, my path in life, and the gospel of peace. I prepare with the good news, that tells me I walk in peace, wholeness, prosperity, shalom, nothing missing, nothing broken in my life.

Above all I take the shield of faith! Which is large enough to cover my whole body, it protects me in front and back, both coming and going. Faith that is a gift of God that I choose to receive, certifying that the revelation God birthed in me will come to pass. This shield of faith will extinguish every fiery dart or plan of the enemy.

Now I put on the helmet of salvation - the salvation that Jesus bought for me on the cross. I receive it and I walk in it now!

I take up my sword, the Word of Truth, to be life to me now and those promises He has given me through the Holy Spirit.

And now as I am armored up for battle I will go out as a warrior of God - in my God given authority. Not letting Satan or his demons to take any ground in my life, or my family's life, my city, my state or my country. I am a warrior for God and He has already won the victory! I cannot be defeated!

TEN: YOU ARE A *VISIONARY*

DECREE: God has put His faith and wisdom in me. He has created me with a dream and passion for my life. I choose to receive His wisdom and guidance to write my own script right now. I will not look back. I press on towards to goal of my vision for my life. I walk in the fullness of what God has created in me, and I take it by faith now! In the mighty name of Jesus, Amen!

ELEVEN: YOU ARE A *WARRIOR*

DECREE: I am a mighty warrior! I am trained for battle. God arms me with physical, mental, emotional and spiritual strength. He enables me to stand on the mountain tops. He sustains me and He stoops down to make me great. He arms me for battle and makes my enemies bow at my feet. I will overcome all my enemies.

TWELVE: YOU ARE *VICTORIOUS*

DECREE: I am always victorious. God has made me victorious over all the works of Satan. I walk in victory as I stand in faith with the word of God! I am living in a victory parade! God locks arms with me and goes with me to fight off my enemies. I always overcome and win the victory. I choose to live by faith in the word of God and not give up. I keep fighting the good fight of faith. I will not grow weary. I will run and not faint. I will prevail with God.

THIRTEEN: YOU ARE FULL OF *WISDOM*

DECREE: I pray that the Lord Jesus Christ, the Father of glory may give me the spirit of wisdom and revelation in the knowledge of Him. I pray, *the eyes of my understanding being enlightened; that I may know what is the hope of His calling, what are the riches of the glory of His inheritance in the saints, and what is the exceeding greatness of His power toward us who believe, according to the working of His mighty power which God worked in Christ when He raised Him from the dead and seated Him at His right hand in the heavenly places. Amen (Ephesians 1:17-19).*

FOURTEEN: YOU ARE *JOYFUL*

DECREE: I am full of joy! I have the Holy Spirit inside of me and He has supplied me with the gift of joy. I choose to walk in that joy. I choose joy today, over any other feelings that may try to come up inside me. I choose to walk in the fruit of the Spirit. I make a quality decision right now to put God first place in my life and go to Him when I have needs. I will walk in the fruit of **JOY** today.

FIFTEEN: YOU ARE *PEACEFUL*

DECREE: I choose to dwell in peace. I choose to allow the peace of God to rule my heart. I choose today to take a solid stance on the Word of God that says I can live in peace. I take that! I accept God's peace. I ask you Holy Spirit to teach me and to give me wisdom on how to walk in peace. I ask that you fill me up with the fruit of peace today. I choose today to put my life in the right order and to put you Jesus and Your Word and Your Spirit first place in my life. Amen.

SIXTEEN: YOU ARE *BLESSED*

DECREE: God is able to make all grace, every favor and earthly blessing to come in abundance to me, today! I will have complete sufficiency in everything and be completely self-sufficient in Him. I will have abundance so that I can give on every occasion. I choose today to walk in God's prosperity, abundance, health; physically, emotionally and spiritually-- all of God's blessings. I will not walk in the counsel of the wicked (those who walk in unbelief) or follow their advice. I will delight in the law and precepts or the Word of God.

SEVENTEEN: YOU ARE *RIGHTEOUS*

DECREE: I will make it a priority in my heart to pursue You and to be filled with Your righteousness. Create in me the desire to make You first place in my life Lord, and I will take the steps to do it. Show me the value of putting my relationship with You first in my life. I will choose to realize You only have my good in mind and in our relationship. You will always bless me abundantly, and I choose today to receive it. Thank you for Your gift of righteousness that I could never fulfill by myself. Thank you for loving me so completely, I choose to walk in the righteousness!

EIGHTEEN: YOU ARE *COURAGEOUS*

DECREE: I will be courageous! I will meditate and believe the Word of God. I will believe what the Word says about me and my circumstance. I will not be moved by Satan or his lies. I choose to go with God. BUT MY GOD! He will save me; He will deliver me from the hands of the enemy! He will never leave me or forsake me. He is my tower of strength in all circumstances. I will prevail with God on my side. I will be a courageous warrior and fight the good fight of faith. I will win!

NINETEEN: YOU ARE *STRONG*

DECREE: I am strong in the Lord. I draw strength from the Lord and His truths. I have a strong spirit, that is rooted in the Word of God will sustain me in bodily pain or trouble. The Lord is my strength and I will run and not grow weary! I will walk in strength and the truth of God's word and be steadfast as my rock foundation. I will overcome all attacks from the enemy. I will win!

TWENTY: YOU ARE *FAITHFUL*

DECREE: I receive God's gift of faith right now, today. I choose today to un-wrap His gift, the Word of God and to be built up in His most Holy faith. I will hear and keep hearing the Word of God. I choose this day to walk in the gift of faith. I choose this day to do the work that it takes to put in the Word of God in my life.

TWENTY-ONE: YOU ARE *SIGNIFICANT*

DECREE: I am raised up with Jesus and empowered to walk in freedom and power on this earth. I am significant! God the Father and Jesus the Son see me as significant! I am empowered to do the works that You, Jesus, did while on the earth. I am loved by Jesus enough that He choose to die for me to buy my redemption. I am seen by God and my life is significant!

TWENTY-TWO: YOU ARE *FREE*

DECREE: I choose to accept Jesus as my personal Savior and receive the freedom He bought for me on the cross. I choose to walk in freedom today from the curse of the law, from selfishness and from sin. I will choose love today. I walk in freedom from the curse, from sickness, disease, depression, hopelessness, worry, lack and death of any kind. I walk with the Holy Spirit and in the freedom and liberty of Christ.

TWENTY-THREE: YOU ARE *UNOFFENDABLE*

DECREE: I choose to remain unoffendable! I choose to walk in forgiveness trusting that God has this! He will bring favor and goodness to me in every situation. He will take care of those offending me. I trust Him to have my back! I choose to trust God and let go of the hurt today!

TWENTY-FOUR: YOU ARE *HOLY*

DECREE: I am set apart for God's use, to bring the message of love and peace to this world. I will choose to walk in purity and make moral decisions to live my life. I choose to walk set apart for His purposes, sanctified and blessed. I will be dedicated to God, His Word and His ways for my life.

TWENTY-FIVE: YOU ARE LOVED

DECREE: God loves me so much! He thinks about me and every detail of my life every day, every moment. He loves me so much He wants to be involved in all of the details of my life. I will spend time sitting with God today and leaning into Him in order to realize how much He loves me.

TWENTY-SIX: YOU ARE FILLED WITH *GRACE*

DECREE: Father God, thank you for your unmerited grace/favor pouring over my life. I am blessed beyond measure; above all I can dare ask or think. I freely receive God's grace/favor in my life. I choose to un-wrap the gift of grace you freely want to give me. I will spend time with the Holy Spirit so that He can make me aware of God's favor in my life today!

TWENTY-SEVEN: YOU ARE *ROYAL HEIRS:*

DECREE: I am a joint heir of the Royal Priesthood of God. I share Jesus' inheritance with Him! I choose today to walk in my inheritance as someone special, set apart and holy. Thank you for blessing me and valuing me! I will walk in that knowledge today!

TWENTY-EIGHT: YOU ARE *CHOSEN*

DECREE: Jesus I choose You today and I will choose you tomorrow! I am a chosen one dearly and deeply loved by God the Father and Jesus the Son! I love you Lord and accept you as my personal Lord and Savior over every single aspect of my life. I CHOOSE YOU JESUS! I choose to walk in the fullness of everything you paid for at Calvary. I will walk as a chosen one and walk in the light of God's love.

Contact Information

You can contact Su Gilstrap at:
Website: https://www.Sugilstrap.com
Email: Su.Gilstrap@sugilstrap.com

Other materials are available on my web site:
www.Sugilstrap.com
You can also find me on
Instagram @sugilstrap
Twitter: @GilstrapSu
Like us on Face Book at: Su Gilstrap

www.ingramcontent.com/pod-product-compliance
Lightning Source LLC
Chambersburg PA
CBHW060839050426
42453CB00008B/753